HOW TO IMP

A

HIGH SECURIT

IN THE H

By

Joel M. Skousen

Third Edition

First Edition 1994
Second Edition 1998
Third Edition 2009

Contact and Ordering Information

Author: Joel M. Skousen
290 West 580 South
Orem, Utah 84058
(801) 224-4746

email: joel@joelskousen.com
Website: www.joelskousen.com

ISBN: 1-56861-054-8

TABLE OF CONTENTS

IMPLEMENTING A HIGH SECURITY SHELTER IN THE HOME 1
INTRODUCTION 1
DESIGN CRITERIA 2
1. Fire 2
2. Natural Disasters 2
3. Crime, Intrusion, Theft 2
4. War (Nuclear, Chemical, Biological) 3
5. Financial Crises 4
FLEXIBLE DESIGN 5
A NOTE ON PRIVACY IN CONSTRUCTION 5

CHAPTER ONE PLACEMENT AND LAYOUT CONSIDERATIONS 7
The Optimum Layout 7
Downsizing to the Minimum 8
OPTIMUM MINIMUM SIZE 9
ABOVE GROUND CONSIDERATIONS 10

CHAPTER TWO HS SHELTER FEATURES AND FACILITIES 12
LIVING FACILITIES 12
SLEEPING AREAS 12
STORAGE 13
BATHROOM 13
LIGHTING 14
VENTILATION 14
Ventilation for Chemical and Biological Agents 16
Fire Survival And Ventilation 17
EMERGENCY ESCAPE EXIT 18
WATER SUPPLIES 20
SANITATION 24
Radiation Sanitation Notes 25
ELECTRONIC SYSTEMS 26
ALTERNATE, INDEPENDENT ELECTRICAL SYSTEM 28
Wiring 29
EMP PROTECTION 30
RADIATION METER 32
RADIATION EFFECTS SUMMARY 34
NOTE ON ECONOMIZATION 36
COST ESTIMATE 38

CHAPTER THREE HOW TO BUILD YOUR HS SHELTER 39
Structural Considerations Wall and Ceiling Structural Elements 39
Ceilings 40
Walls 40
Main Door 41
Foundation and Floor 41
STEP BY STEP INSTRUCTIONS FOR CONSTRUCTION 42
STEPS OF CONSTRUCTION: 43
FINISHING THE INTERIOR 49

Exterior Finish 49
Concealed Entrance Construction 49
Construction of the Battery Vent Chamber 50
Electrical System Schematic 51
Ground System 53

CHAPTER FOUR 54

HOW TO FORTIFY A CLOSET 54

DESIGN AND LAYOUT CONSIDERATIONS: 55
DIFFERENT LEVELS OF SECURITY CONSTRUCTION: 57
STRONGER WALLS 57
STRONGER DOORS 58
DOOR JAMBS AND LATCHES 58
THE LOCKS 59
OPTIONAL DOOR BRACES 59
THE CEILING: 59
CONSTRUCTION TIPS 60
WALLS 60
INSTALLING GRAVEL: 61
CEILING 64
VENTILATION: 64
DOORS: 64
CONCEALED CABINET 66
DOOR CROSS BARS 66
....

APPENDIX:
A. Source listing of Equipment and Suppliers
B. Comprehensive List of Items to Stockpile
C. Suggested Barter List
D. Water Purification and Storage
E. Installing a Reserve Water Tank in the Home
F. Installing a Cistern
G. Nuclear Radiation Protection Proceedures
H. Consulting and Design Services

IMPLEMENTING
A HIGH SECURITY SHELTER
IN THE HOME

INTRODUCTION

Most people who have been away from home on an extended vacation have a universal question on their mind as they return: "I wonder if everything is OK at home." Some are even reluctant to leave a home unattended simply because of the potential theft of irreplaceable items. Alarm systems are an important, but only partial answer to this growing concern. There is still the problem of long response times in many cities–time for an expert burglar to be in and out before the police arrive.

Suppose you travel in business, and your family lives in a hurricane zone or in a tornado region. You are out of town and a powerful storm system strikes your area, or even an earthquake (which can happen anywhere, even if you aren't close to a fault line). Telephone lines are down and the airport is closed. You would feel rather helpless being hundreds or even thousands of miles away not knowing the fate of your family.

All of these and other potential threats are real. But there are solutions that can help you find greater piece of mind in this world full of problem people and unpredictable events. This special report outlines how you can provide a much higher degree of safety for your valuable assets and your family's lives when you construct a high security vault room in your home.

The enclosed plans and specifications provide all the essential details you need to know about in constructing a MULTI-PURPOSE, HIGH SECURITY SHELTER (HS Shelter) within your existing home. While this report will emphasize working within an existing home or structure, the same design principles, with some modification in details and specifications can be applied to new construction, if you are planning to add on to your existing residence.

This HS SHELTER is, in reality, a **fire proof, seismic designed, VAULT ROOM with self-contained emergency living and storage facilities**, complete with **independent power and water supplies, filtered air, communications, and a concealed, secure entry.**

In Chapter Four, I also detail for you the much cheaper option of fortifying a Master Bedroom wardrobe closet. You may even want to implement this option along with a HS Shelter elsewhere so that, during an intrusion, you and your wife have a mini secure room to retreat to for temporary security.

Design Criteria

The basis for design of this shelter is related to five common threats: FIRE, NATURAL DISASTER, CRIME, WAR and FINANCIAL CRISES. I believe every family has a high probability of confronting at least 3 out of these 5 within the next ten years.

1. Fire

With modern building construction techniques, the probability of suffering a major fire is diminishing. However, because it is relatively inexpensive to fireproof a small vault room, and the benefits are so high, I have included this feature in the HS shelter. In order to safeguard essential personal belongings, records, and valuables, the shelter is designed to survive the complete destruction of the surrounding house by fire. Depending upon the location of the shelter within the home, it also allows for family members trapped within the home to seek refuge within its walls and remain protected from smoke and heat, for at least 2 hours.

2. Natural Disasters (EARTHQUAKE, TORNADOES, HURRICANES)

The shelter is designed to withstand winds in excess of 200 mph and the resulting collapse or destruction of the house around it (which is probable in winds in excess of 120 mph). Thus, the HS shelter makes an excellent tornado shelter, and is also designed to act as a semi-autonomous, rigid cube in an earthquake. It will retain its strength and form as it "floats" amid the movements of the house surrounding it–thus providing complete personal protection during the disaster itself and temporary living quarters throughout periods of utility disruption that follows.

3. Crime, Intrusion, Theft

The shelter is a maximum security vault capable of withstanding all but the most expensive and determined types of forced entry. Nothing within the realm of most family's finances is capable of being completely safe from forced entry, given enough time and equipment on the part of the criminal. The purpose of this project is to provide such a high level of expense and deterrence **for the criminal** that he will seek other targets of opportunity. This security room also acts as a personal shelter for family members who do not wish to confront an intruder with personal defensive weapons. From inside its walls they can communicate with sources of outside help by telephone or radio. A concealed entrance is one of the most formidable ways to deter sophisticated thieves from casing your home, posing as a repairman or salesperson. In addition one cannot discount the historical threat that governments themselves have posed in confiscating private assets, weapons, artwork and even food.

4. **WAR** (NUCLEAR, CHEMICAL, BIOLOGICAL)

The HS shelter is designed to provide you a protection factor of 32 against nuclear radiation, as well as blast shielding as close as 5 miles from ground zero if the shelter is in a basement location and as close as 10 miles if above ground. The radiation protection factor indicates that the designed shielding will reduce incoming radiation to 1/32 of what you would receive outside, unprotected. This is sufficient to avoid most effects of radiation sickness. A basement location will at least double your protection level for the walls. Most importantly, the shelter is equipped with radiation monitoring so that you can determine when it is safe to come out.

Most US citizens living at least 15 miles from a major military base or military communications and control facility will be spared the physical devastation of the blasts. However, almost every person will be subjected to the long-term sickness associated with exposure to nuclear radiation, carried by the winds. In addition, there is the potential of large scale damage to electrical systems and computerized components everywhere through exposure to Nuclear Electro-Magnetic Pulse (EMP) attacks that always preceed a nuclear war. These are high altitude nuclear detonations which destroy electrical equipment through electro-magnetically induced **high voltage surges** in power lines and electronic equipment.

Why be concerned about the nuclear threat if government and media sources have assured us that Russia is no longer targeting the USA with its long-range missiles? First and foremost, I don't believe it. Even if it were true, it takes less than 15 minutes for an enemy to change back to the old targeting data. Secondly, there are dozens of other terrorist nations and their surrogates who are developing small nuclear weapons with Russian covert assistance (North Korea, Syria, Iran, India and Pakistan and others) that may become a direct threat in the future. Third, China now also has long range nuclear missiles capable of hitting the western half of the US, and our government in 1998 agreed to begin supplying China with advanced missile technology capable of increasing both range and accuracy. Fourth, despite all the media hype to the contrary, there is a great deal of credible evidence that the so-called demise of the Soviet Union is more illusion than fact. In the appendix at the end of this special report, I have detailed many of the arguments and facts that explain the background to this grand deception and what possible outcomes you may expect and plan for.

The bottom line is that the Russians and Chinese are cheating on all fronts of the disarmament game: n**uclear, biological, and chemical warfare**. Their secret production facilities are still off limits to inspections. Defectors claim their governments are working overtime developing new weaponry--and that they still intend to strike. Don't believe all the hype about Soviet disarmament. Nuclear missiles in the "former republics" are not being "dismantled and destroyed" as US media report, but rather are being dismantled and *transported back to Russia for stockpiling and reloading on newer missiles*, all at US taxpayer expense. In short, all evidence points to the fact that the Russians still plan on launching a crippling nuclear strike on US military targets, without warning, sometime in the future. I suspect their ultimate goal is to take Europe without a fight, and they have to remove the US as a military power before they can sufficiently blackmail the Europeans into submission. Personally, I think it is a few years away–the Russians still have a lot of technology they want from naive western nations, but they will strike when the proper provocation presents itself.

Even if you disbelieve or discount the nuclear threat, it is relatively cheap insurance to proceed with the preparation of this shielding capability, since the structural mass is serving several other security purposes at the same time. Do not, however, become fatalistic or complacent about the oft heard idea that, "We're all going to die anyway in the nuclear war, so why should I try to protect myself ?" Some will die from radiation exposure, it is true. But it is an agonizing death, and there are almost no medical procedures or training to stop or even alleviate the symptoms–if you could even get access to medical help. Remember that none of our hospitals have made any provisions for nuclear war, thus guaranteeing that health professionals will be sick or dying just like the rest. But worse than dying is the fact that most people will survive in a most rudimentary way, suffering long-term illness and effects for years to come. Believe me; you don't want that kind of agony. The good news is that protection against radiation is relatively simple to achieve. So, why rely on the untrustworthy pronouncements of Russian leaders? Whether they now call themselves "reformed Communists" or "Socialists", they are the immediate followers of those who terrorized the world for decades, and who are still providing covert support for terrorists, Islamic fundamentalists, Bosnian Serbs and a host of other enemies of liberty.

5. **FINANCIAL CRISES** (PERSONAL BANKRUPTCY, BANK FAILURES, OR DEPRESSION)

While the HS shelter cannot actually provide shielding from financial depression itself, its integral, self-sustaining sources of power, coupled with long-term stockpiles of food, parts and household supplies, will eliminate or at least postpone your needs for money in the short term while you maneuver to provide alternative sources of income. Stockpiling is a very effective form of insurance and secure savings, and can even take on some aspects of an investment if barter items are stored. Barter items are things which become highly sought after in a time of shortages. Comprehensive listings of suggested stockpile and barter items are included in the appendix.

Flexible Design

The plans and designs included in this report center around a standardized 2-chamber shelter, built from reinforced concrete block construction–the type of construction most suitable and readily available for do-it-your-self construction. However, suggestions for implementing larger multi-room shelters are also provided, as well as details for alternate forms of construction which may be more suitable for new construction. If you need a customized design for special circumstances I am available to help on a consultation basis as also detailed in the appendix.

Finally, you may find that your assessment of the dangers facing you does not necessitate constructing a large enough facility to shelter people, but only valuables. If you desire to build only a vault room, you may be able to reduce the size of construction down to that of a large reinforced closet. Chapter Four, new to this edition, will help you reinforce a walk-in closet to serve as a semi-secure safe room near your bedroom. With this compromise alternative, you can still achieve a high degree of fire-proofing, and intrusion protection. If your needs for secure storage are less than 30 cubic feet, then you would be better off simply buying a home floor safe such as those built by Liberty Safe Co. Liberty Safe now builds Remington and National Safe brands as well.

A Note on Privacy in Construction

If you have the time and skills, or are capable of learning the skills (not difficult), I recommend you build this vault structure yourself. You can save at least half on construction costs, and gain the advantage of complete privacy as well. If you have to hire it done, try to find an experienced, old fashioned, reliable handyman to do it. Using a big name contractor with lots of temporary construction workers is an invitation to having your plans noised about freely. Don't ask your handyman to bid on something so unconventional as this. Make sure he is a good, hard worker, and pay him for time and materials. Refer to everything in the structure as a "fire-proof storage room" or "storm shelter"–not as a survival or bomb shelter. The word "survival" has become severely tainted of late. Avoid using the term "vault room" even though this will be an unavoidable conclusion once you install a vault door on the front entrance. You don't want to give the impression you are storing large amounts of valuables. On the other hand, don't try to pass this off as a "root cellar"–it has too many sophisticated aspects in it for this to be credible. You want to de-emphasize the purposes of this unit, while still being believable.

There are a few other tactics you ought to employ in order to safeguard yourself and family against an intrusion or threat of force.

1. Make sure all your children's bedroom doors have locking doorknobs–the kind you can open with a small tool, if necessary, rather than a key. Your own master bedroom door should provide an even higher level of protection since you are the one who needs sufficient safety and time to respond to the threat. Your door should be the solid core type with keyed lock or deadbolt. These precautions prevent the horrible sensation of being surprised at your bedside by the dark form of an intruder–leaving you almost no options.

2. If you have a security system, have it modified so that when an intrusion to your perimeter doors or windows occurs, it doesn't just set off a loud alarm that sends you into a panic. Have a "master enunciator" panel installed in your bedroom that gives you some indication of where the threat is coming from. Some even provide audible responses telling which zone has been violated.

3. Have a cheap portable safe somewhere in a closet in your home, so that if a family member is threatened to reveal the location of valuables, he or she can point out this safe, rather than the vault room. Stock it with important looking papers and a few minor valuables.

4. Have a cellular phone in your bedroom at night so that you can communicate with the police even if the phone wires are cut.

5. Keep a suitable smoke hood or gas mask by each person's bed. In case of a fire (where smoke is the primary killer) you can search out your children without danger of asphyxiation. Older children can help get other children out this way too.

If you have to fight a small fire, you can do so for a limited time using the mask. There is a new and relatively inexpensive smoke hood on the market, made in Canada by Kaptair ($42). It completely covers your head and filters out smoke and noxious gases for up to half an hour. Kaptair is even coming out with a new mask in 1998 that filters out Carbon Monoxide--a real breakthrough. You can order direct by calling (800) 838-5898. Ask for the ExitAir Mask.

CHAPTER ONE

Placement and Layout Considerations

Even though this report is designed specifically for implementation into an existing home, it is instructive to begin with a view of what we could do in an optimized situation (all new construction) where we are not constrained by an existing structure. After a brief look at the optimum, we can then talk about the compromises we will have to make in downsizing a shelter to fit into a basement room or a garage.

The Optimum Layout

The optimum shelter should consist of four separate rooms: a living/eating/all purpose room, a sleeping area, a bathroom area, and a storage area. The simplest design corresponds to a room that fits under a typical two car garage. It measures about 24 feet by 24 feet overall. Placing an 8 inch concrete dividing wall down the middle provides support for the concrete roof span above and allows for two long rooms with interior dimensions of approximately 11 by 22 feet. Each of the two concrete rooms is again divided by a frame wall to provide one small room (about 8x11) and a larger room (14x11). Two of the rooms form a storage room and a bathroom combination. The two rooms on the other side of the main dividing wall become a living area and a sleeping room, as is illustrated below:

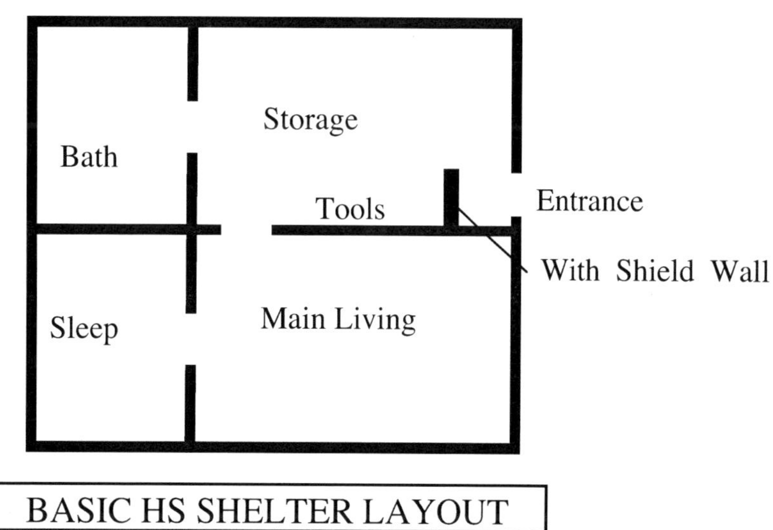

BASIC HS SHELTER LAYOUT

Subdividing the shelter in this manner is important due to the fact that some radiation sickness may be present when people are exposed prior to entering the shelter. Sick, crying, and moaning victims can make for a very unpleasant environment if everyone is cramped together in one small room. Add to this the unpleasantness of toilet smells in the same room, and the potential lack of light and one becomes motivated very quickly to ensure that proper provisions are made for separation of people and that you provide proper equipment. Even in the absence of these physical discomforts, keep in mind that people do not get along well together for extended periods in close quarters, even in the best of times. Providing the opportunity for both group togetherness and privacy separation is essential, when you can afford to provide the space.

You will note that there is a lot of space dedicated to living quarters–mostly due to the possibility of a nuclear attack in the future. However, there is nothing here that dictates you cannot use this space for other storage items in the meantime. You can always move this excess storage outside the door if you need the shelter for living space someday.

In new construction, the ceiling should be built from reinforced concrete, 12 inches thick. A safe reinforcing plan for such a ceiling is to provide a bottom grid of #5 reinforcing bars (3/4" diameter) 12" on center, both ways and a #4 bars 24" on center, both ways just under the top surface of the cement.

Downsizing to the Minimum

Now, let's talk about a less costly, practical design for placement of the shelter within an existing home. In order to provide the maximum protection and privacy, the HS shelter should, whenever possible, be located below ground level and designed into the basement of a house. A basement already provides a high degree of protection from wind storms as well as a reduction of radiation exposure of 10 to 15% (depending upon the size and orientation), even without a shelter. A basement also has better temperature control due to the heat sink qualities of the surrounding earth. For those who do not have a basement and who cannot build a basement (due to unsuitable ground, or ground water conditions), an above ground concrete or masonry structure must be constructed.

Let's first discuss basement options. Depending upon what space you want to give up in a basement, you generally have the option of building a large shelter while still allowing for ease of concealment. Taking a large portion of an above ground garage may be a convenient choice, but it will not be as easy to conceal. In the basement, the best location is at the far end, rather than in the middle, so that you have a least two existing walls to work with. These walls must have no windows, or the windows have to be filled in with concrete block. If you have an area already dedicated as a storage room that may provide a good location for a shelter. If possible, one should also try to build the new shelter around the area where the incoming water supply enters the basement. This gives you first control over water entering the structure and allows you to divert it easily to storage tanks within the shelter. If you have a basement bathroom, it may be advantageous to incorporate it as well, as it provides an alternative access to water and toilet facilities. Obviously, all these factors may not coincide with a single location, and you will have to compromise, or choose between them.

To take advantage of concealment options, it is best to locate the shelter in such a way that the shelter structure occupies an entire end the basement so that the new end wall of the basement makes it look like a smaller partial basement.

OPTIMUM MINIMUM SIZE

The optimum, minimum shape to shelter 4-6 people is a rectangle room:

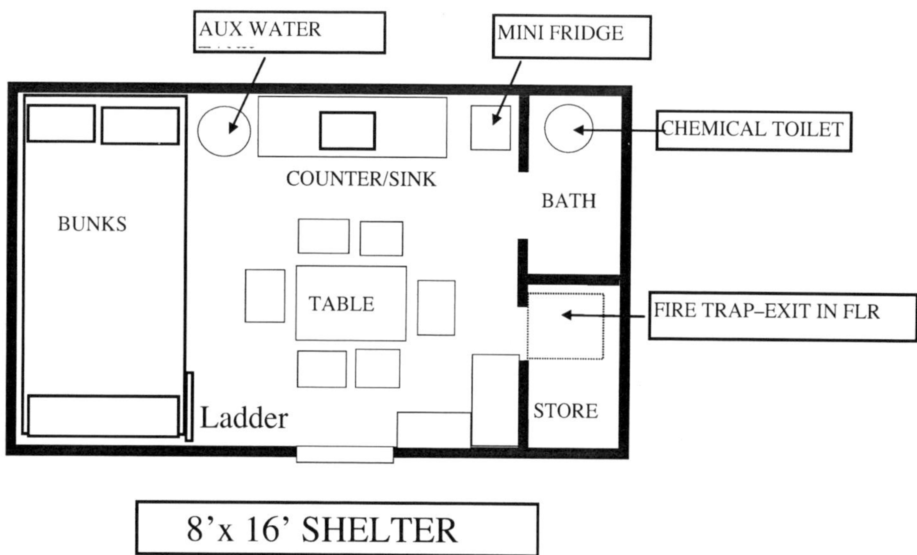

8'x 16' SHELTER

Obviously, if you have more room, you can allow for a larger structure. However, keep in mind that this modular plan is designed structurally for a maximum width of 10 ft. The main steel reinforcement runs in the short direction, thus determining this critical 10 ft. span. A larger length (in the long direction) is allowable without re-engineering, but do not exceed 10 feet in width. The following design change, based upon a 4 foot interior width, allows us to fill out an entire basement wall or to fit a narrow shelter at the end of a garage,

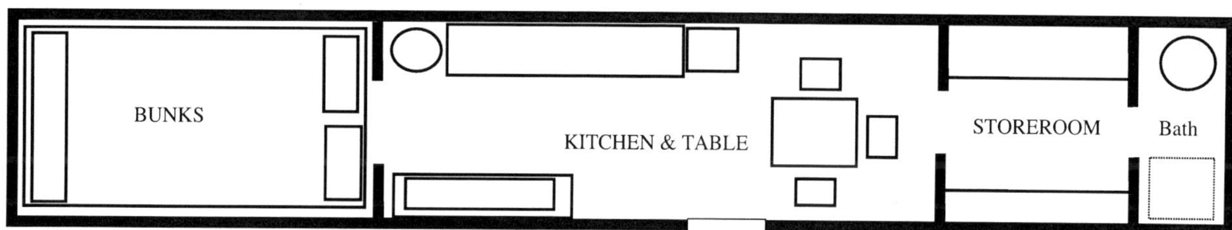

4 X 32 SHELTER LAYOUT

Obviously, there are certain inconveniences in this compromise, such as accessing the bunk beds from the pillow end rather than the side, but it is still very functional. This longer design also requires more intermediate walls for lateral stability of the long walls in a storm or earthquake–but this is not difficult to do. Remember, that you can select almost any shape you want, even L shaped, as long as you stay within modules of 10 feet in width. While vault rooms can easily be engineered for wider widths, it is more costly and more difficult to construct. You must keep in mind that we are going to build this within an existing room, and the ceiling will have to be constructed without having working access from above. The ceiling of the vault room will be designed about 7 feet in height, and will be constructed, of necessity, from the side rather than from the top. So as to avoid problems of excess reach in this construction process, I prefer to stay with a room 8 feet or less, and 10 feet at the maximum.. Don't worry if you don't understand this difficulty right now, it will be explained fully in the section on construction techniques.

ABOVE GROUND CONSIDERATIONS

Because the house itself is usually heavily compartmentalized and optimized for living space, it is difficult to convert some of that space into a vault room without sacrificing utility. The best possibilities for building a vault room (within the house proper) are in an extra bedroom or storage room that can be converted into a "room within a room." The normal entrance door now becomes a linen closet with concealed access to the inner vault behind. This, however, is also only practical if the house is built on a concrete slab which can hold the weight of the vault room. If you have a crawl space, it is usually best to excavate a portion of it to provide a deeper space and locate the HS shelter there (water table permitting).

Do not rule out the possibility of a small addition to the house. If you need an extra den, family room, or office, consider building one with a shelter underneath, or an above ground room only, with the shelter occupying a portion of it. Another excellent alternative is to add on a vault room within the master bedroom complex–usually as part of the closet system. This provides the most convenient way to gain quick, private access to your security room if an intrusion or destructive storm occurs at night while you are sleeping. See Chapter Four for more details.

Concealment is never as good in the above ground option, but often people cannot escape the basic limitations of living in an area where no basement is possible. Now, just because no one has a basement in your area doesn't mean it can't be done. I am amazed that in certain areas, builders simply got it into their heads long ago that, "We don't do basements here," without any real reason other than it was too much effort or too costly (in the old days). Unless you have high water table problems, or solid rock underground, you can build a basement–though you will pay quite a bit more in construction costs than in areas where there are many skilled workers who know how to do a basement economically. Even the two exceptions concerning bedrock and water tables can be overcome with present technology, but it is quite expensive.

For most people, who are not going to add onto the house, the best option is found in the garage. Because the average length of cars is getting smaller (now only 14-16 feet rather than 16-18 feet) and the average garage size is getting bigger (24' x 24' instead of 20' x 20') chances are you have room to work with. The best choice for most will probably be a narrow shelter room along the entire back wall, covered by appropriate storage shelves for concealment, as illustrated below:

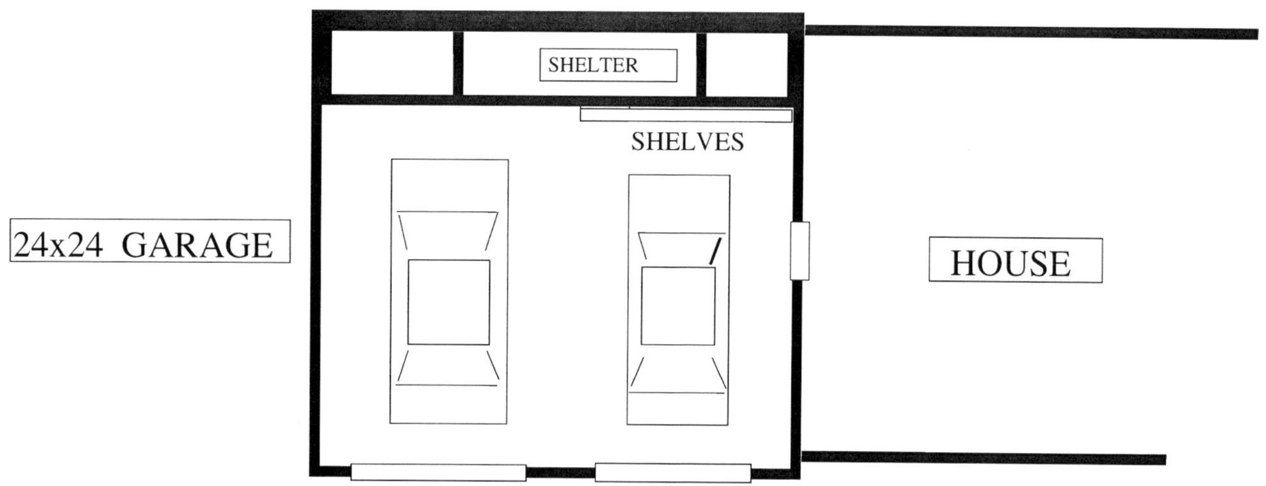

This arrangement assumes a minimum garage depth of 24 feet. The HS shelter is 6 feet by 24 feet, outside dimensions.

CHAPTER TWO

HS SHELTER FEATURES AND FACILITIES

LIVING FACILITIES

Living areas are multi-purpose areas. One needs to provide for cooking and eating facilities–consisting of a small counter and sink, some cupboards or shelves, and a small expandable table with padded folding chairs (when you do a lot of sitting for two weeks, or a month, you'll appreciate the padding). The kitchen should be equipped with utensils, dishes, pots and pans, a mini microwave oven, a small 5 cu. ft. refrigerator (GE or Sanyo make units which run on only about 100 watts). You should also have a two or three burner propane gas camp stove with four 5 gallon propane cylinders. Also provide a propane catalytic-glow heater if you live in a cold climate–mounts on the top of a propane cylinder. These don't produce CO but use a carbon monoxide detector to ensure safety. In larger shelters, you may also want to provide a hide-a-bed type sofa for comfortable seating that can double as a bed at night. A small administrative counter and chair is nice to have to operate the radio, telephone, TV/Stereo/VCR, and security system, and to record the results of periodic radiation readings. Bookshelves for reading material should also be provided.

SLEEPING AREAS

A separate, dedicated sleeping area allows for more privacy and quiet than makeshift foam mats placed on the floor. Some shelter designs with small dimensions utilize single bunks hinged to the wall and suspended by chains or cables so they can be folded out of the way when not in use. This type of arrangement should only be used when space is extremely limited and must be used for two or more purposes during the day. In a real life radiation emergency, the chances are high that some members of your family are going to be sick and need to stay in bed all day. It is quite inconvenient to have them sleeping on the floor in a traffic area where they are constantly disturbed, or on a bunk hanging right over a kitchen counter, for example.

The sleeping area I have designed is just big enough for one set of triple bunk beds made from 4x8 sheets of plywood. These double wide beds are inherently more efficient than single bunks since hallway access space is nearly eliminated. This arrangement will sleep 6 adults, two to a bed, and give room at the head or foot of each bed for storage of personal items. It will sleep more children, who take up less space. These bunks can be left in place at all times or used as storage shelves. They can also be built so that the bunk bed plywood bottom is detachable from the support rails (bolted to the walls) so that the full space can be utilized until the bunks are needed. Hinging these large sized bunks is not recommended, as they are too big to go up flush against the wall, vertically.

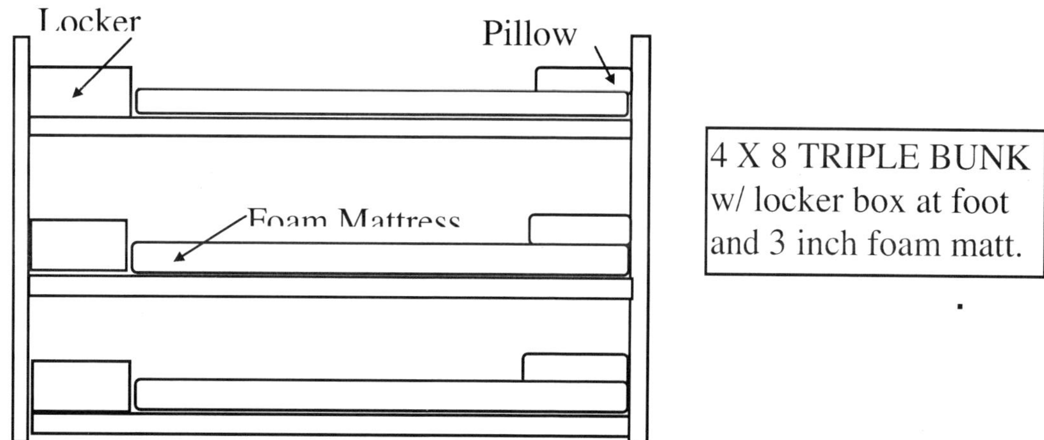

STORAGE

If you store everything I have listed in the comprehensive lists at the end of this report, you may well fill up the entire shelter and leave no room for living. It is important to store in the shelter all the essential items that you will need, to live for a month. This will leave plenty of room to store valuables and other sensitive equipment that you may want to safeguard permanently or simply when going on vacation. A full-sized shelter would have a large dedicated storage room, but in smaller shelters, you may be limited to a large closet area or to shelves on the living area walls–or even stacked boxes on the floor. A storage room may not only include shelves for stored food and supplies, (and possibly the water tanks if the main water line enters or passes through this room), but also a heavy-duty work-bench-type counter to provide a small work area with tools. This ability to fix, build and repair items while in the shelter is invaluable. One must make provisions to cover all contingencies possible, within space and budgetary limitations.

BATHROOM

In a full-sized shelter, the bathroom should contain a bathtub/shower combination if room permits, a hand pump marine-type toilet or at least a chemical toilet and a deep sink which doubles as a bath vanity sink and a laundry/first aid sink. The first aid and medical supplies should be in this room as well, so that any treatment of radiation sickness can take place away from the normal living area.

In smaller, minimal shelters, there will only be room for a chemical toilet. You can either buy one of the many types available through sporting goods houses, or make one yourself from a 5 gallon plastic pail and a cheap toilet seat. Lysol and other aromatic disinfectants diluted in water are suitable substitutes for commercial chemical toilet liquids. Bathing in minimal space must be done by sponge baths, so it is important to provide some privacy even in the smallest shelters. Exhaust ventilation will also exit the shelter from this toilet area so that unwanted odors do not drift into living areas. Naturally, air intake vents should always enter the main living areas first and exit via the bathroom.

As a plumbing note, all gray water (sink and bath water) should be saved and used for the chemical toilet, in order to conserve fresh water for drinking and culinary needs.

LIGHTING

Although kerosene lamps should be stockpiled in case your 12 volt electrical system fails or runs out of storage capacity, these are not my first choice in lighting due to the odor and slight smokiness emitted. The Aladdin type lamp is smokeless, and puts out as much light as a 100 watt bulb–but it also burns a lot of fuel. Propane lights are comparable to electric lighting, but it is important to conserve your propane supplies for cooking, whenever possible. Since propane, like the kerosene lamps, also burns oxygen, more ventilation is needed to compensate.

The optimum sources of lighting are 12 volt fluorescent type fixtures. The model #197 units from **Thinlight** Corporation are ideal. They have a self-contained switch and lens cover and come with a super efficient electronic ballast connected to a 36 inch long fluorescent light tube. They cost about $75 each, however. A more modern alternative for point lighting are the new 12 volt white **LED lights** that use about ¼ the current. One good source is **ITC Incorporated ~ 230 E. Lakewood Blvd., PO Box 8338, Holland, MI 49422-8338 Phone: (616) 396-1355** http://www.itc-rv.com/led.html Also check local availability at camping stores, RV dealers, sporting goods stores, or discount variety stores.

Provide standard 110 volt lighting throughout as well, but make sure you also provide a separate junction box inside the shelter, for these lighting runs. This way, if house power is not available, you can disconnect the wires at this junction box, connect the lights to your 12 volt system (be sure and have extra wire on hand), replace the normal light bulbs with 12 volt bulbs (Abraham Solar can provide these–see sources lists) and you are back to normal.

VENTILATION

The shelter must be capable of excluding all potentially dangerous fallout particles, and provide some exchange of fresh air to sustain a healthy atmosphere. This is especially important where sickness and odors are present and when oxygen burning appliances are used for lighting, heating, and cooking. Anytime you have a lot of people occupying a small space for several weeks, bad air and odor are bound to become a problem. The entire shelter system should have a minimum of four vents; two air intakes that are filtered and two exhaust vents. The intakes should come into the living and sleeping rooms and the exhaust should exit from the storage or the bathroom. This provides the freshest air to the living areas and ensures that bath odors exit from the bathroom. The following conceptual drawing illustrates the construction of one type of vent for a basement shelter that draws air from a wall in a room above (more detailed drawings in the plans section). Filtration on the inlet pipes is provided by fastening one or more circular HEPA or even an auto filter to the wall of the room above (where the vents originate) over the pipe elbow that comes out of the wall. Filters must always be <u>outside</u> the safe room. Use silicone caulk or glue, as it provides an air-tight seal and yet can be easily removed when the filter needs replacement. When the filter is in place on the wall over the pipe inlet, glue a circular piece of cardboard over the opening in the face of the filter, thus forcing all incoming air through the filter material on the sides of the filter.

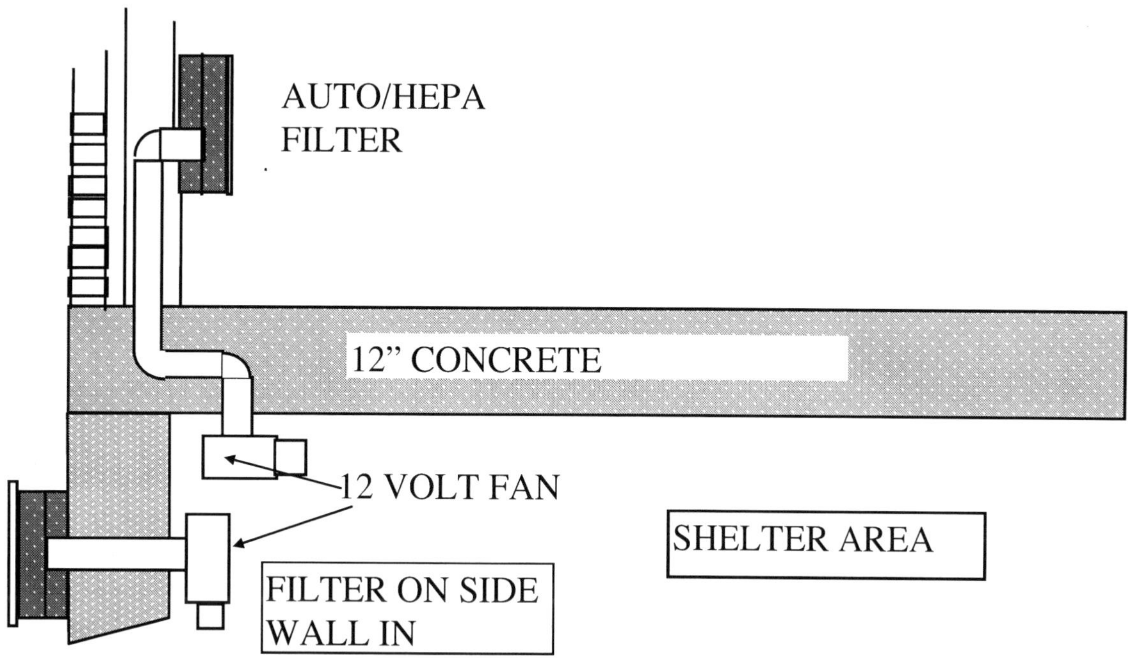

There are many different placement possibilities for vent and filter locations. The above drawing has indicated two of them. The one on the top is for a shelter built under the garage slab and uses one of the garage walls in which to conceal the vent pipe and mount the filter (preferably in a cabinet for concealment and protection). The one on the left of the drawing represents a side-wall mount, which may be used in a shelter constructed within an existing room with a ceiling. If you build a regular steel or wood framed wall around your concrete walls, for concealment purposes, the filter can be mounted on that wall and penetrate directly into the shelter. The use of the auto filter is sufficient for shelters where the house will not be subjected to blast effects. In this way, the house itself acts as the primary filter, thus allowing us to use a very economical and available filter unit.

You will have to make the decisions as to where to place the vent holes since these will depend upon where the room is placed relative to other structures. Here are some guidelines:

1. Plan on 2 inlet vents and two exhaust outlets. Battery vents will be considered separately.

2. The preferred location of inlet vents is low toward the floor for above ground shelters. This allows for the coolest air, as well as the best chance of smoke avoidance.

3. For fallout pre-filtration, it is best to take inlet air from an existing room–either the room the shelter is located in, or an adjacent room. In this way, the house acts as the first filter against fallout particles, which is quite effective when windows are intact.

4. For concealment of the filter elements, they are best located in the rear of some form of cabinetry. The shelf system concealing your entire shelter wall is ideal for this purpose.

5. For basement shelters, the inlets can come from the basement itself or from a room above, if you can gain access to a wall above, without too much remodeling difficulty.

6. If you make provisions for an emergency exit underground, make allowances for an air intake there as well, in case of fire (further explanation later in this report).

7. Almost without exception, plan on exhausting the outlet vents to the small air space between the new shelter ceiling and the existing ceiling of the room in which the shelter is constructed. Do this along the rear wall. The strategy here is to avoid the detection of sounds that are channeled out vent pipes. There is no way to get an ear even close to outlet vents located in these positions.

Ventilation for Chemical and Biological Agents

There is no more sophisticated type of filtration than that required for chemical and biological agents. CBA (chemical-biological agents) filters combine a chemical absorbing media (usually carbon, potassium and zeolite) with an ultra fine particle filter (down to .3 micron). Chemical and biological agents are growing threat, even though they haven't been used extensively since W.W.I. There is increasing evidence that our soldiers in the Gulf War were subjected to small amounts of chemical or biological warfare, resulting in the numerous medical maladies. Terrorists have been given access to these agents by various communist governments. There is also the very disturbing account in a recent article in Reader's Digest of one Russian defector's account of new, secret biological warfare agents being developed in Russian–a flagrant violation of the recent accords. The fact that the West has had large stockpiles of chemical weapons has had a strong deterrence effect against the use of chemical weapons by the Russians or other surrogates. But since we have now been unilaterally disarming and destroying our stockpiles, that deterrence is lessening in the same way the nuclear deterrence is disappearing.

A dedicated CBA filter is very costly to buy (around $8000 plus shipping). The Swiss LUWA filtration system is fairly large (about half the size of a 55 gallon drum–plus accessories) and contains not only an air pre-filter, and CBA filter, but blast valves, electric positive displacement fan, a handcrank fan, case and mounting brackets. A positive displacement fan is necessary because of the high back pressure or resistance a CBA filter creates. You have to force the air through it, since the filtration medium is so compact. The filter canister comes with a special seal. Do not break this seal until ready to use, otherwise the CBA filter takes on moisture over time and may lose some of its effectiveness, or become contaminated with bacteria.

This unit must be mounted inside your shelter so that the handcrank handle can be turned. I do not recommend using the electric motor since the air volume is too high for the needs of a small shelter. CBA filters have a specified life of some 2000 hours under motorized volumes of air. This can be extended dramatically by only using the hand pump which pumps a much smaller volume of air–but which is more than sufficient.

The CBA filter must draw its air through a prefilter on the outside of the shelter. We do not want fallout particles to enter this Swiss CBA filter unit which is (stupidly) placed inside the shelter. Even though the fallout particles would be trapped by the CBA filter, they would radiate the inhabitants of the shelter from the filter canister (the radioactivity will pass through the thin metal filter container, even though the particles are contained inside). This is why we place all air filters outside the shelter walls, so the fallout particles remain outside. The sole U.S. distributor of LUWA filters is Utah Shelter Systems listed in the Appendix. They also provide prefabricated Steel Culvert blast shelters for outside burial--highly recommended if you must remain in a blast zone (which is *not* recommended).

Now I realize that most of you cannot afford this kind of expense just for filtered air, critical as it may be to your survival. So here's a vastly cheaper way to substitute an off-the-shelf American made filter system which is nearly as effective. Hospitals and Allergy patients use special HEPA filters that also come with a Carbon/Potassium/Zeolite filter for trapping chemicals. These can be purchased in a variety of shapes and sizes. I discovered that the Honeywell filters for the model #63200 (and other) units are cylinder shaped just like the auto filters we are using, only deeper and bigger. Stacked together and installed on the wall outside the shelter in a similar manner as the auto filters just described, these filters will give you the protection you need--and the cost is about $180. See the Sources Appendix for ordering details.

Fire Survival And Ventilation

Air filtration and venting in case of fire is a more difficult proposition. Even though the shelter will not burn or collapse around you in a normal fire, it will get very warm inside, despite the interior insulation–although it will take well over an hour to begin to penetrate the masonry heat mass and insulation. In almost all cases, where help would arrive within an hour or two, one could survive inside without any ventilation at all. But in a prolonged case of fire, one must be prepared to withstand the oven effect as the masonry mass of the shelter slowly heats up to oven temperatures and penetrates the insulation over time. Remember, insulation doesn't stop heat infiltration, it only slows it down.

For this reason, we design a pit under the concrete floor within the shelter. One should design one of the vents to come from the outside, under the house, and into this pit so that a constant source of cool, fresh air comes into this pit at all times. Thus, even if the shelter itself heats up after an hour or two, it would be tolerable for those in the pit. As an ultimate precaution, this pit, with an appropriate tunnel, can lead to the outdoors where one could escape. But for security reasons, this exit must not be open, or accessible from the outside, except when actually needed. This will be covered next under EXITS. For this underground fire vent to be effective, it must be open to the air far enough away from the house as to not draw in smoke or carbon monoxide from the fire itself. There is no cost-effective filtration against carbon monoxide. To accomplish this, we must draw in air away from possible smoke. If at all possible, it should exit at a place where the land drops off from the level areas of the yard. This way, smoke currents, which normally swirl around on level ground, will begin an upward movement at the point where the ground drops off. This has the tendency to keep a steady stream of fresh air flowing past the vent intake. If there is a prevailing wind direction, place the intake toward that direction. None of this is foolproof, but it vastly increases the potential of survival in a fire.

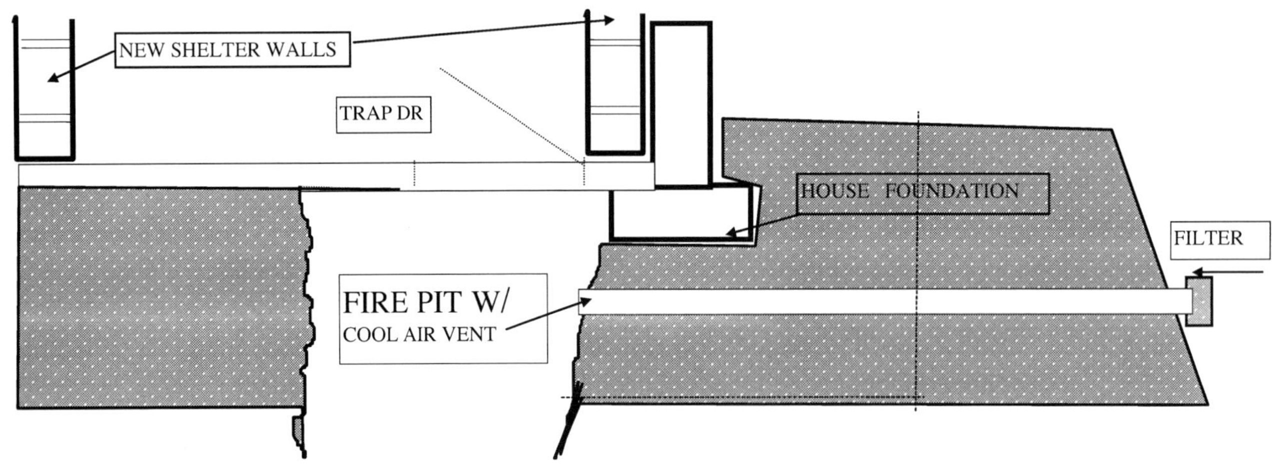

EMERGENCY ESCAPE EXIT

This exit can be an extension of the safety fire pit, tunneling under the foundation to the outside as illustrated by the dotted lines, and terminating in a sand trap exit (to be discussed later). In general, you need not fear tunneling under a short portion of the home foundation. Footings and foundations have sufficient steel reinforcement to withstand 2 to 3 feet of undermining. But you should not tunnel any distance horizontally once outside the house, without shoring up the tunnel ceiling and sides with metal or pressure treated plywood and lumber to guard against cave-ins. Even if you think it is unlikely, you must always consider the possibility of an earthquake (which can happen anywhere). The under floor exit just described is the preferred exit for above ground shelter construction.

There are many different ways to conceal exits as they emerge from the ground. One of the best is to have one of your local air-conditioning contractors provide you with a used shell of an old evaporative cooler or of an air-conditioning unit. Instead of pouring a normal concrete pad as an outdoor base, pour one with a hole in the center for your tunnel exit. Then attach the shell of the air conditioner over it, with one side hinged, and with a suitable inside locking latch so that it can only be used from the inside. With filter screens in place, the entire exit tunnel can serve as an air intake. The only drawback to this arrangement is that its concealment is not foolproof. The only truly foolproof way to do that is to provide an exit that does not penetrate the ground until use. Such an exit is described below. The best of both can be incorporated by having a sand-trap type of exit under the air conditioning shell. This way, when it is used, the newly opened exit is still not visible to others (since the hole is concealed under the cooling shell).

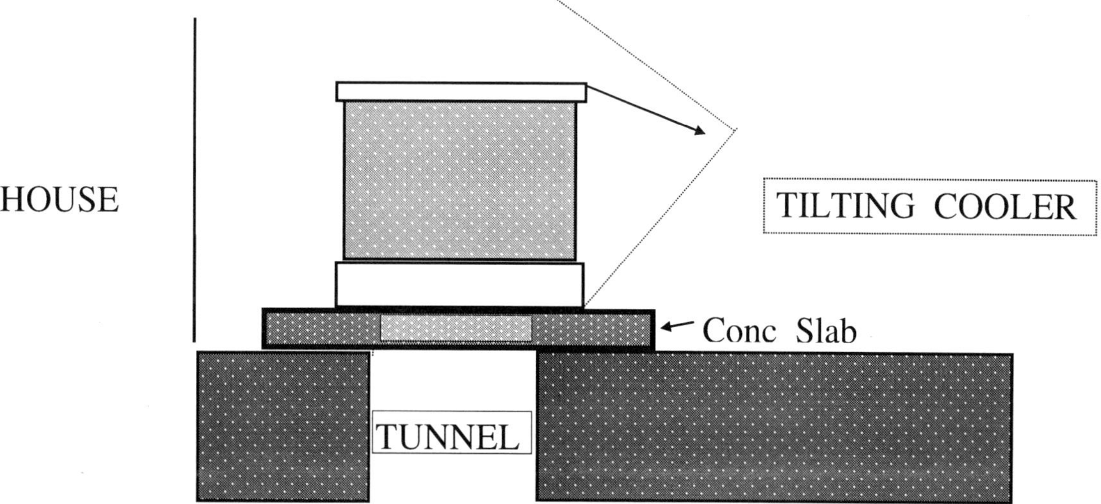

The next type of exit is a wall exit, suitable only for below-ground construction, and can be located on any convenient wall that provides access to the exterior land around the house. The most economical and secure exit is a "**sand trap**" exit, as detailed below: A small opening (at least 2 ft. by 2 ft. and no bigger than 3 ft. by 3 ft.) is made 1 foot off the floor of the shelter in the outer concrete wall. This can be sawed out with a concrete cutting diamond saw if one was not provided in the original construction. An excavation is made on the outside wall and two corrugated metal window wells are stacked one on top of the other on the outside of the basement, reaching from the footing to 6" below the ground level. A treated piece of plywood is cut out to the inside shape of the window well and installed at the top (resting on a horizontal 2 x 4 that spans the top of the window well next to the concrete wall) and a couple of "break-away" 2x4's placed vertically inside the window well (see next illustration). In this way, one edge of the plywood is capable of falling inward into the well space when the brace is broken. This movable side is kept in place by break-away supports as shown. It is then covered with thin 2 mil plastic sheeting and covered with sand, and a few inches of dirt where it joins the normal ground line. The entire unit is then filled back in with dirt so that the sand trap exit is completely concealed. Open it by pulling out the break-away supports, letting the plywood roof fall inward. Do not stand directly underneath as you do this. The sand and plywood will lie in the bottom area of the window well and assist you in climbing out. Prior to usage, it is not possible to detect since it is covered with sand and earth outside. It can even be covered back up after use by retrieving the plywood and reinstalling it, covering it up with earth.

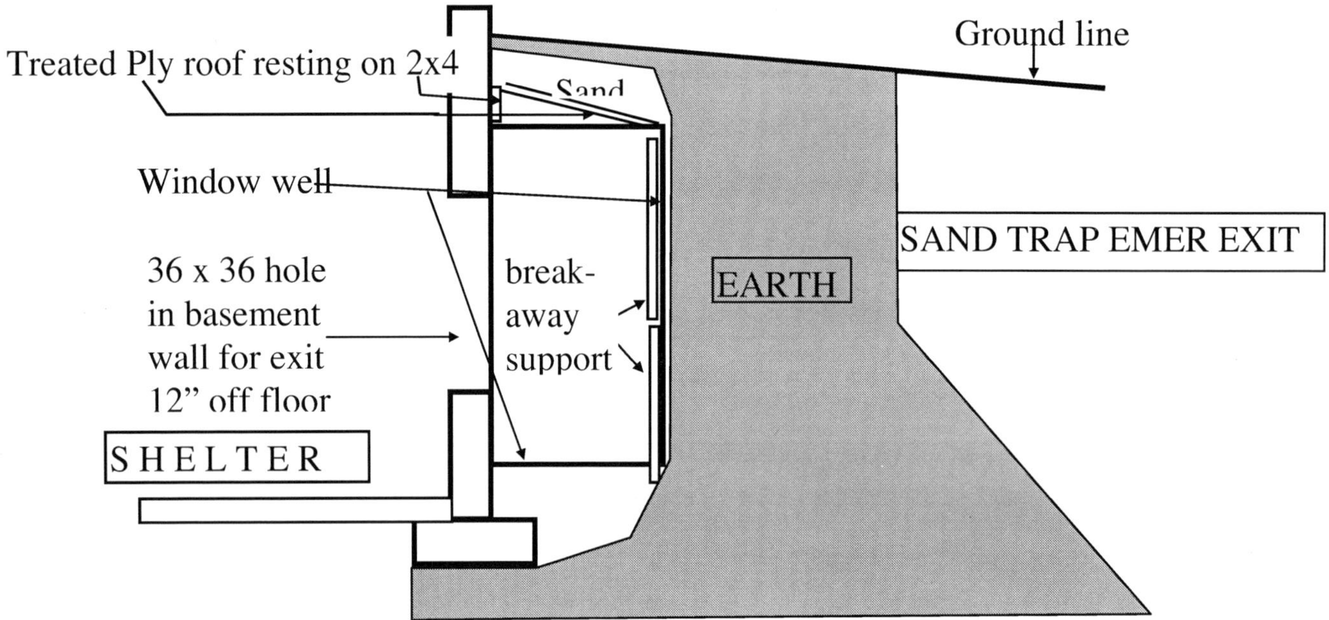

WATER SUPPLIES

As a minimum, you can simply store water in plastic water barrels, but it is much more secure to have a cold water pipe tapped into the shelter as well. If you do use static storage of water, treat it with an oxygen purifier like Aerobic K07, which is described later in this report under the heading of **water purification**. Your water should remain potable indefinitely if cool and dark. All other types of water purification leave a bad after-taste or chemical residues in the water which are not healthy.

I rarely recommend you try to bring conventional hot water into a shelter. It is doubtful in most catastrophic crises that your normal source of hot water would be available to you, unless you have a passive solar water heating system (which I recommend if you can afford them. The KingSolar brands are both excellent in quality www.kingsolar.com).

In new construction, your house plumbing system should be designed so that your incoming main water line should enter through the portion of the house where the shelter will be located, so that you have absolute first control over the water source from the shelter. It is also preferable that the sewer pipe should exit through or just outside the shelter so that shelter waste lines can easily be attached. It is not necessary to have plumbing in the floor of the basement. A sump pump can be operated from your alternate electrical system to pump sewage up to the sewer line, and marine toilets are available that are operated by a small hand pump capable of pumping up at 6-8 feet in height. In the minimal type of shelter we are discussing in this report, you will probably not go to the additional expense of tearing up the foundation to install a sewer. Instead we will store sewage in 5 gallon buckets, or plastic garbage cans with air tight lids for later disposal.

To ensure a supply of storage water that always remains fresh, it is best to plan on installing an in-line water storage tank inside the shelter. "In-line" means that your tank forms part of the line from your main source of water to your household fixtures. This way you will continually have fresh water flowing through the tank when other normal household fixtures are being used. For this reason, an in-line tank must be capable of withstanding normal house water pressures (up to 150 psi). In contrast, a static water storage tank is a non pressurized holding tank and would have to have the water changed every six months to ensure freshness (unless antibacterial agents are added such as Aerobic 07).

However, caution must be used in using an in-line storage tank. One has to be careful that contaminated city water does not get into your in-line storage tank (as is possible in an earthquake) when lines will be broken and the siphoning effect will draw dirt and debris into the water system–perhaps even sewer water from broken sewer lines lying in the same trench. None of this will enter your house automatically, but if you begin to use water from the city supply after an earthquake, you could bring in contamination. By the time you notice dirty water coming from your faucet tap, your tank is already contaminated, since it was "in-line" with your tap. As a precaution, close the tank inlet valves and open the bypass valves on top of your tank after an earthquake (see In-Line Tank plumbing diagram in the appendix). This ensures that the water already in the tank will not be contaminated, and still allows you to draw water from a tap until contamination appears. The reason for drawing water after a quake is to fill a bathtub or other large container with wash water for emergency use, in anticipation of loss of water pressure.

Additional precautions can be taken by installing an inexpensive set of in-line sediment and charcoal water filters on the main water line just prior to the storage tank. These are readily available at almost all home builder stores. These filters will not clog under normal city water use, but will partially safeguard your supplies initially from dirty water which may enter in a disaster.

If your city water system gets its water from any open sources of water (lakes, rivers, etc.), it is probable that such sources will contain fallout during a nuclear incident. Do not let such water enter your home. The water itself is unaffected by radiation, but it may carry into your water system radioactive particles floating in the water. If your city system relies upon large electric pumps, you may not have water available, even if uncontaminated; due to damage to the electric utility grid by an EMP strike (Nuclear Electromagnetic Pulse from high altitude explosions, to be explained later). City water systems that come from wells or covered springs and stored in covered holding tanks could also be contaminated, if the venting systems draw in air containing fallout–however, this would represent very small amounts, and would be filtered out in your shelter pre-filter. Pre-filters should be checked daily during a nuclear incident by your radiation meter for sudden increases in radioactivity. Remember, it's only the particles that originate from the airborne dust of a nuclear explosion that are radioactive. Things radiated by gamma rays do not become radioactive.

One or two new or used 50 gallon water heaters make an excellent in-line water storage tank for the shelter. If you have an electric water heater as your normal source, install a propane heater as the auxiliary source. If you have natural gas as the normal source, install an electric tank. This way you can ensure an alternate source of power for your water heating needs. In electric models, one can even replace the heating elements with 12 or 24 volt varieties and heat water with the excess electricity from your solar panels (see alternate electrical section). Larger tanks are available at a higher cost. Water heater tanks have the advantage of having a drain at the bottom with a hose attachment. This allows you to conveniently extract water from the tanks when there is no water pressure. Be sure and have a small 5 ft length of garden hose available to attach to the drain. Otherwise the outlet is too low to the ground to drain into a decent sized container.

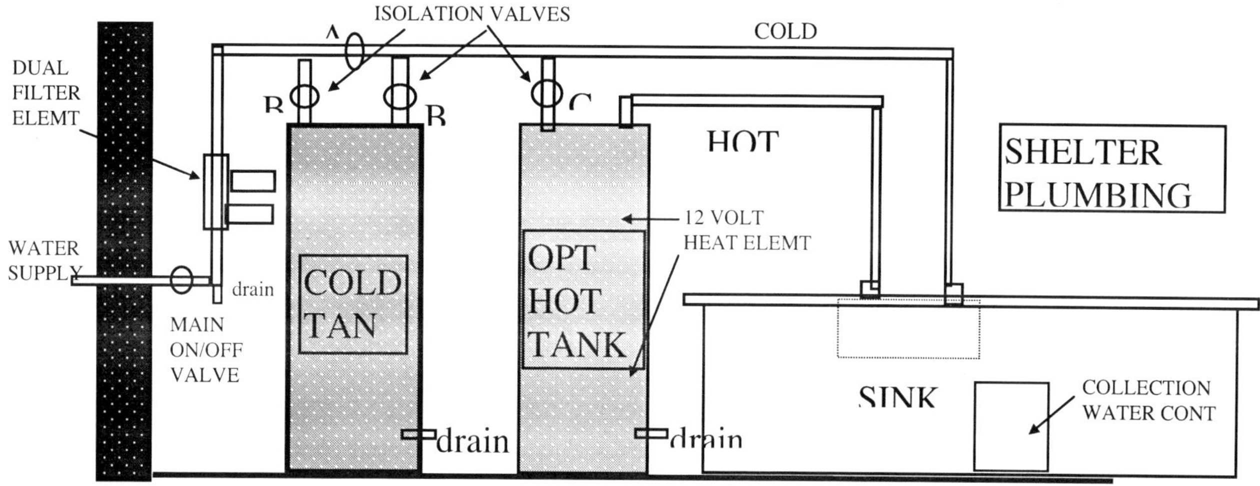

The above plumbing diagram shows both a cold water in-line tank and an optional warm water tank which would be heated by excess 12 volt electric heat from the Photovoltaic solar panels. The electrical portion will be explained later. The important thing here to understand is the use of the isolation valves. The drawing shows the main water supply entering the shelter. This may be directly from outside, if you build your shelter where your water supply normally enters the house or basement, or it may represent a new line you have brought into the shelter from elsewhere in the house. It should have a main shut-off valve placed just after the line enters the shelter plus a drain valve where the pipe begins its upward turn. This allows you to drain the entire system which is sometimes necessary when making repairs.

Next comes the **dual filter element**: a fiber pre-filter (sometimes called sediment filter), followed by a charcoal filter.

From here, the water goes on toward the first tank. There are three **isolation valves** here (regular lever-handled manual ball valves) which control whether you choose to make the water flow into the storage tank or bypass it. To keep a fresh water supply in the first tank (designated for cold water), close the valve marked "A" and open both valves marked "B". This sends all the water through the tank before it goes on toward the next tank and the sink. If you had an earthquake and wanted to make sure the storage tank is not contaminated by incoming city water supply, you would close the "B" valves and open the "A" valve. If dirty water eventually begins to come out the sink faucet as you use water, then shut off the main shut-off valve. Now you are limited to what water you have stored in both tanks. This is accessed by opening the sink faucet to allow air to enter the system as you drain one tank and then the other via the lower drain valve. If you suspect the water in the top pipe feeding the tanks has been contaminated, open the drain valve next to the main shut-off (which must be closed by now). This, combined with opening the cold faucet on the sink will allow all the water in the main feed pipe to drain out before you take water out of the storage tanks. If you do not do this, some of the contaminated water in the top main feed pipe may drain down into the storage tanks as you empty them from below.

The **hot water tank** is optional. It is good to have a heat sink to which you can divert the excess electricity generated by your photoelectric solar panels. After the batteries are charged up, your charge controller will automatically switch the sun-generated electricity to the 12 volt heating elements you have installed in this second tank. It won't be a lot of electricity, but it will warm up the water after a few hours. In any case, whether the water gets warm or not (depending on the sun and how much charging goes to the battery) it is always available as a supply of extra drinking water.

Another alternative installation is to suspend one of the tanks from the ceiling with suitable hardware capable of holding at least 300 lbs in an earthquake. This would involve 14 inch long bolts that went all the way through the ceiling and 1" wide by 1/16" thick metal straps. When attached to your shelter sink, you now have gravity fed water available at the faucet. Use 1/2 inch polyethylene plumbing lines in the shelter. They are flexible, easy to install, and earthquake and freeze resistant, unlike rigid copper or PVC plastic pipe.

The drainage from the sink goes directly into a bucket underneath. This is stored for use in flushing toilets or making disinfectant liquid for chemical toilets. Several sets of plastic 5 gallon buckets with lids should be kept in the shelter for storing and handling liquids and wastes.

SANITATION

In new construction of a house, which includes a shelter design, it is best to have installed a **regular toilet** using either a gravity sewer connection or a sump-type, ejector/grinder pump to elevate sewage up to the sewer lines above. Even if water pressure is not available, a toilet can be flushed with residual bath, laundry or kitchen wash water. Remember, however, it takes at least 2 gallons of waste water to pour into a regular toilet bowl to start the flushing action. So it is wise to restrict flushing to once or twice a day to ration your waste water. Leave the regular lid and seat up after use and cover the bowl with a makeshift, tight-fitting cover that will lock in odors more completely than a regular toilet seat. Even plastic wrap will do the job.

In a long term shelter situation where water is critical, it is best to have a **marine toilet**. (Jabsco makes an economical model available at Yacht or Marine supply houses). These units are built for sea-going yachts and have a small hand pump unit which simultaneously pumps water out of a bucket of waste water sitting nearby (which you provide) into the bowl and then up a pipe connected to your sewer line, or even into another covered waste bucket. If you line a bucket or small plastic garbage can with a heavy duty garbage bag, you can seal up the bag when full enough and remove it for disposal or storage, allowing you to economize on the numbers of containers needed for sewage collection. If you pump up to a sewer line, use no larger than 1-1/2 inch ABS plastic pipe to lead up to your sewer connection to ensure the column weight of liquid is minimal. The weight of the water in larger diameter pipe is too much for the hand pump to handle. If you have a sewer connection or holding tank installed below the level of the basement, you will not have to worry about lift. To ensure you have an ample supply of waste gray water for flushing the marine toilet, pipe the drain water from the kitchen sink or bath vanity to a 5 gallon plastic bucket directly underneath and inside the cabinet. If your shelter has access to underground sewer lines, you can drain the overflow from these wastewater buckets by cutting (near the top of the bucket in the side wall) a tight fitting hole for ABS drain pipe. Seal with silicone and connect to the regular drain in the wall or floor–wherever it is located. This essentially makes the bucket into a huge P-trap when the lid is on the bucket and sealed tightly. Another half inch polyethylene line can then be run from the bottom of the bucket, up through a small hole in the lid and over to the marine toilet, so it can be pumped by the toilet pump into the bowl for flushing.

A **portable chemical** toilet is another suitable, but less convenient alternative, due to its limited quantity of disinfecting chemical and the need to transfer or eliminate the waste via plastic bags, from time to time. On the positive side, it is the most convenient, economical, and simple to install--despite its limitations. Even if you decide to install one of the more sophisticated toilet systems above, its good insurance to have at least a make-shift chemical toilet on hand as a last resort, as described below. Make sure you have plenty of 30 gallon garbage bags on hand for sanitation purposes. Even if you run out of chemical, you can make substitute disinfectant with waste gray water, Lysol and/or Pinesol brand deodorizer/cleaner.

The **homemade chemical** toilet is made from an empty 5 gallon plastic bucket with a toilet seat sitting on top. Inexpensive plastic toilet seats can be purchased at any home builder's type of store. Make sure you obtain a small regular toilet seat, not an elongated one, in order to properly fit the top of the bucket. Place a small sized garbage bag in the bucket, add one gallon of waste water mixed with a 1/2 cup of Lysol or Pinesol brand disinfectant, place the seat on top and it is ready to use. When not in use, lay the seat aside and replace the bucket top to keep odors in (but do not snap the lid down tight as they are fairly difficult to get off).

Radiation Sanitation Notes

In a full-sized shelter with room for a normal bathroom, the bathtub/shower is essential for performing a washdown on family members who may come into the shelter after being exposed to actual fallout. The freshly radiated particles, if trapped in a person's hair or around the openings in clothing, can cause dangerous beta burns if not removed immediately. Train everyone beforehand how to react if caught in the outdoors when fallout begins to rain down. They should cover their hair, nose and mouth with any clothing they are wearing so that particles are not lodged or ingested. They should avoid contacting the actual particles in the air at all costs, and get to cover as soon as possible. It is easy to discard clothing which may have fallout on it, but impossible to get it out of the lungs once inside.

It is essential that fallout not enter the shelter, thereby defeating the protection of the shielding. Have them leave outer clothes outside the door, enter quickly, shower down and dress in new clothes. Make sure you have an extra supply of clothes in the shelter of varying sizes for just this purpose. Old sweat suits are ideal as they are baggy, and loose–easy for almost any body to fit into. Make sure you have extra undergarments of all sizes in storage as well. Toss any contaminated clothes out the door–do not try and wash them–the exposure is not worth it until they have lost almost all radioactivity.

If you have a minimum shelter, of the type we are designing here, you may not have room for a shower, although small fiberglass showers are available that measure only 30" by 30". One of these could be tucked into any number of designs we have thus described. Because the waste water from showering could contain fallout, one should cut a small hole in the concrete floor underneath and dig a pit in the earth (at least 2 feet deep) to eliminate the waste where it will not radiate the others in the shelter. Use an elevated bucket or a camper's type shower (a plastic bag with a small a small flexible plastic drain hose attached to the bottom for a shower head. It uses a small clamp to shut off the flow as needed).

In a small shelter, without full shower or bathing facilities, hair can be washed using the main sink, and other parts of the body washed in the privacy of the small toilet enclosure with a sponge or washcloth. Remember, however, that water must be strictly rationed, even when you have 100 gallons of storage. Get fellow inhabitants used to the idea of not bathing very often, if at all, and (more difficult yet) of using wash water numerous times before setting it aside for toilet water. It is very difficult to know in an earthquake how soon water will be restored. In a fallout emergency, just as your readings may reach a level where you think it may be safe to exit the shelter, the high altitude winds may bring a fresh dose of fallout from further west. When you get down to 4 gallons per person, there should be no more washing–only drinking and cooking water. When you reach 2 gallons per person, you should save it only for rationed drinking water, and eat very, very little. Eating takes more water than normal in order to digest the food.

Electronic Systems

Each shelter should have provisions for telephone, radio, doorbell and intercom equipment, even though some of these may not be operable (like telephone) in all types of emergencies. (Specific recommendation on what to buy and where are listed in the Appendix).

An **intercom** and a **door bell enunciator** are essential in order to speak to people pounding on your house or shelter door (if discovered) who may want information or access during an emergency. It may not be safe to actually open the door once you are inside your shelter during an emergency–for security or fallout reasons. The intercom should be of the type that allows you to listen in on other rooms in the house. This remote monitoring capability is essential in an intrusion or other situations to determine accurately what is going on. If you seek shelter in the vault room during a criminal intrusion, it is nice to be able to direct the police by your secure telephone or radio to the area of the house where you have heard the intruder.

Additionally, it is important to have a remote **master control panel, or enunciator panel** from your home **security system** inside the shelter so you can monitor the security status of the home above, and take appropriate action.

All control panels for your alternate electrical system should be located inside the shelter so they can be monitored and/or repaired when necessary.

A **telephone** should be provided inside the shelter so you have access to the most convenient form of communications. If you have a cellular phone, install one in your shelter with a small external antenna, otherwise the cage of reinforcing steel in the shelter walls will deter some of the cellar phones transmit power from getting out.

For last resort, sure communications, you should have a combination 2 meter/440 **amateur radio** installed. This is capable of transmitting to both ham radio operators and some fire and police frequencies. In certain emergencies, the ham radio people will be your only means of effective communication with the outside world. It is not very difficult to secure a ham radio "technician" class license, which does not now require learning the Morse code.

CB (Citizen's Band) or **Family Band radio** is a cheaper alternative, and does not require a license. However since these uncontrolled frequencies are so overused by persons transmitting with power in excess of the legal maximum, you may find it difficult to talk to anyone. CB Channel 9, however is reserved for emergencies, and is monitored by all police units. This is the channel you would use in an emergency anyway, and it would not have the kind of interference you find on other channels. You can get a 40 channel CB radio at most electronic stores for less than $75. Family band radios are even cheaper now.

Television and VCR are nice options which help alleviate "cabin fever", being cooped up in tight quarters for days on end. Television news coverage, if available, will be a partial source of news, if stations are in operation.

The **world band, short wave radio** is your only dependable source of reliable news in the worst emergencies. This is because you can tune into far away places, such as Europe or South America which may not be affected by the crisis in the US. If you know a foreign language, you will get much better access to news than if you are limited to

English. The news media in European countries is far better than US sources at telling the truth. The BBC newscasts in English are fairly good, much better than USA's Voice of America. Radio Havana and Radio Moscow operate big programs in English, but it is predictably full of propaganda and noticeably lacking in any negative comments relative to socialist and communist maneuvers around the world. The Germans and the Dutch put out excellent English language broadcasts, as well. Get a copy of the latest edition of "Passport to World Band Radio". It contains essential frequency information so that you can find the locations and broadcast times of your desired stations (order by phone from AES or HRO Electronics, listed in the appendix).

There are a lot of excellent short wave radio receivers on the market. The two all-around best brands in performance and price are Sony and Grundig. I personally carry Sony's newest production miracle: the SW100S–a full world band receiver in miniature–the size of a cassette tape! I carry it wherever I travel. It has the latest in new technology, excellent sound, lots of accessories, numerous memory channels, and tells you the time anywhere in the world. AES or HRO has the best price.

For tabletop portables, I recommend either the Sony SW7600 or the Grundig YB400, or similar updated models. These represent the best performance range for the price.

While all of these portables have built-in antennas, you will have to provide an <u>external antenna</u> because of the shielding the shelter provides. Both AES and HRO sell small portable antenna you can set up in your home attic to increase reception. Or you can simply buy a spool of 20 gauge solid copper insulated wire at Radio Shack and string up a 40 foot long piece around the top corner of the room you want to use as a listening area (outside the shelter). Attach this wire to the antenna on your radio (just wrap it around the tip tightly) and it will increase your reception dramatically.

Alternate, Independent Electrical System

It is highly probable that conventional utility power will be intermittent or out of service for periods of time ranging from a few hours to weeks or months. Tornadoes and hurricanes can cause extensive damage to above ground power lines. Earthquakes are capable of tearing apart even underground trunklines, and destroying distribution and control buildings. Nuclear EMP strikes (to be explained shortly) are capable of destroying vast areas of electrical distribution with such powerful surges that many months would be required to replace control equipment. And even when power was restored, a large portion of sensitive electronic equipment (previously connected to the utility power) would not now function. So, it is clear that alternate electric power must be provided to the shelter. To be forced to stay in a windowless shelter for weeks without light and minimal electrical power would be very unpleasant.

While a generator is a necessary and convenient way to provide short term power, one cannot operate it from within a small shelter due to exhaust fumes, noise, and requirements for fuel and air. I have designed larger shelters with special facilities for generators, but this is not practical here. In fact, your power requirements inside a minimal high security shelter are sufficiently small that a battery backup system, solar charged, and coupled with an inverter is all that is necessary.

The basic system is composed of a minimum of four (4) 18 volt photovoltaic solar panels (75 watt output) which are used to charge eight (8) 6 volt golf cart type deep storage batteries (lead acid type) via a Sun Selector 30 amp charge controller that is capable of diverting the solar charging current to another use when the batteries are fully charged. Lastly we will use a **Trace/Xantrex** brand inverter to convert some of this battery storage from 12 volts DC to 110 volts AC current. These new sine wave inverters do this conversion very reliably and efficiently, and use very little current when not being drawn upon. We will need AC (alternating current) to run radios, the mini fridge, television, security system, intercom, some power tools, and perhaps even small sewage ejector pump, if installed. While some of these items can be purchased to run off of 12 volts (like radios) others, like the mini-refrigerator, run better off of 110 volts ac. Having the inverter handy allows you the option of taking various household appliances (like your wheat grinder) into the shelter with you.

The PV solar cells will be mounted on a portion of the roof via some fairly heavy duty copper cables. The large size of the cables is not necessary because of a high current flow, but to reduce the voltage drop over the distance between the solar panels and the batteries. When you only have 17 or 18 volts to start with and you must charge the batteries to over 14 volts, you cannot afford to lose 3 volts in the transmission process. Larger wires of many strands reduce this voltage drop, or loss. These cables will lead into the shelter and attach to the charge controller and from there will lead to the ventilated battery bank which should be kept as close as possible. The battery bank is then connected to the inverter which is inside the shelter, but not in the same compartment as the batteries. It has its own plug-in receptacles to which you can attach the household appliances you desire.

Wiring

Make sure the following electrical wiring provisions are brought into the shelter:

1. 110 volt house power. This provides you with electrical power for lights and plug receptacles for normal use of the vault room. This electrical source may even be available during some emergencies, such as when tornadoes or hurricanes are approaching.
2. (2) #4 gauge stranded copper cables from the roof mounted solar panels to the shelter. These will provide charging electricity for the emergency backup electrical system.

3. (2) #00 gauge stranded copper cables, color coded black (neg.) and red (POs) from the battery bank compartment either inside, or on the floor outside your shelter, to the connection point where the inverter is mounted. The large sized cables (w/ fused disconnect) are necessary to handle very high amperages the inverter is capable of drawing from the batteries.

4. (2) RG-8x coax antenna cables from (1) scanner antenna in the attic or roof and (2) a dedicated short wave antenna, or long wire wrapped around the ceiling corners.

5. TV ant cable from TV antenna or dish

6. FM radio ant lead, if your home has an FM antenna

7. 12 volt wiring to each room for 12v lights and to power any 12 volt appliances

8. Security system cable from main master panel (Check specs on your system to determine how many pairs of wire are required to activate a remote master panel–which is a panel that can arm/disarm the system and give you indications of intrusions zones activated)

9. A security camera coax video cable (if you choose to install cameras to monitor outside of house, or outside the shelter (optional, but very handy if someone is trying to get in or find you, against your will).

10. Telephone wire and telephone jack outlet (unless you use a cell phone).

11. Doorbell connection (To let you know when someone is at your house door)

12. Intercom connection (A remote master panel with listen-in capabilities).

13. Heavy-duty copper ground wire from water main or grounding system. This is necessary to attach to surge protectors which you must install to protect your electronic equipment from EMP damage. If your house grounds are not closer than 10 feet, drill a hole in the cement floor and drive in a new ground rod. Keep it wet from time to time with a solution of water and Epsom salts to increase conductivity. All shelter electronics are grounded here.

Use #12 Romex wire for 110 volt circuits, and #10 Romex for 12 volt circuits.

EMP Protection

Provide high speed surge protectors for all electronic equipment (rated at less than 10 nanosecond response clamping time). PolyPhaser Corp has dedicated EMP rated protectors but are much more expensive. Use for high value items like computer or radio.

Because of the probability of multiple EMP attacks that will precede a surprise nuclear attack, one cannot expect to receive any US information from radio or television sources for many days. You will have to rely on world band short wave radio sources.

EMP stands for electromagnetic pulse. Technically, we are concerned here with NEMP–Nuclear electromagnetic pulse. Russian and Chinese nuclear attack plans call for several large nuclear weapons to be detonated miles above this country which produce large electromagnetic pulses in all power lines, antennas, and even in normal house wiring.

These high voltage pulses are sufficient to blow out most sensitive electronic components, if not protected. An EMP pulse rises much more rapidly than most electrical surges. Thus even most lightning protectors won't react quickly enough. To be effective, a surge protector must react to shut off the surging current within 10 nanoseconds (1/100th of a microsecond, which is 100 millionth of a second.) Most modern strip plug/protectors, which are widely available and relatively inexpensive, will shut down the spike in less than 2 nanoseconds. Other strip plugs, such as sold in Radio Shack stores are equally as good. Just make sure the specification on the back indicates a reaction time of less than 10 nanoseconds. Whole house protectors (PolyPhaser) are available for installation at your electrical panel, but the cost is high (ranging from $250 to $800). See Sources in the Appendix.

Your first warning that a nuclear attack is imminent may be the visible effects of an EMP strike: a general electrical failure in all parts of your city, preceded by a flashing of your lights and other electronic equipment (especially a TV connected to an antenna), which then burn out, or otherwise fail to operate, due to the surge. You can buy electronic alarms that warn you when the power is out. Use the warning to awaken the family and get into your shelter before the missiles arrive. An Emp strike will generally precede the actual attack by at least 20 minutes. Use a battery powered radio to check if radios are off the air before heading for the shelter. This will help you distinguish between a regular outage and an Emp strike, which will take out radio station antennas. Antennas can be protected by a grounding block adapter (from Radio Shack) which is placed in-line between the antenna and the TV. The grounding block is then attached to a separate ground wire leading to a nearby electrical ground rod or metal water pipe. Do not use the grounding wire in your normal electrical wiring—it will pick up EMP. Better yet, keep antennas disconnected.

Do not count on using computer controlled vehicles for critical transportation after an EMP strike, unless you have a spare. It is possible and even probable that most modern cars with electronic ignition systems will receive fatal damage to the computer ignition system. Only older (pre-1983-5), non computerized cars or non-computerized diesel vehicles can be relied upon to operate after an EMP attack.

High frequency radio antennas are especially susceptible to EMP voltage surges because they are built to pick up electromagnetic waves. They must be protected by special in-line surge or shunt type arrestors, connected to a special high-efficiency ground system.

PolyPhaser Corporation and ICE Corporation make special **surge arrestors for protecting the entire house wiring** from surges that may come down the main power lines. The in-line types are more expensive (about $800) and need to be repaired after a strike–but they provide absolute protection. The less expensive shunt type arrestors (about $250) may let some of the surge pass through, but function again and again. This is because a shunt connection has to sense the surge and then switch on an alternate path to ground. But the electricity still has a tendency to want to follow the larger capacity wires on into the house. The shunt types also are slower than the in-line types. But the shunt connection is the more cost effective in my estimation since your small surge protectors will provide backup protection on individual equipment for any lesser surges that get past the main shunt connector.

No EMP protection equipment is effective however, unless it can effectively divert the electrical surge to ground. In the shelter, this will be accomplished by **establishing a new ground** system and tying it directly to the city water supply line (if it is copper or galvanized iron pipe). If a metal water pipe connection is not available, we will drill a 3/4-inch hole in the concrete floor next to the wall nearest to where most of your electronic equipment is located. Through this hole, we will run a hose of water for about an hour to thoroughly soak the ground underneath. Then pour a couple of gallons of water mixed with Epson salts down the hole. These salts are non-corrosive, but greatly enhance the conductivity of the ground. Next drive a six or eight foot long copper grounding rod down the hole. To this rod we will clamp a 1" wide woven copper grounding strap and attach the other end to a copper, aluminum or even a steel plate, measuring at least 24" by 24". This plate will serve as the mounting plate for EMP protection equipment and serve as an attachment area for the individual ground wires that come off the back of each piece of electronic equipment.

The steel reinforcing cage built into the shelter will absorb very little of the pulse coming directly from the atmosphere, because of the high frequencies involved. Even so, the larger danger will still come from the pulse that is induced in long electric power lines, and comes into your equipment that is plugged into the wall outlets. So keep them unplugged when not in use. If the electrical cord is detachable from the back of the unit, keep it detached until use. Even a six foot cord hanging out of your equipment can pick up enough of a surge under certain EMP conditions to ruin a computer chip. For complete protection keep radios and sensitive electronics in a metal box that is grounded.

Special care must be taken to make sure each radio, telephone, and TV antennas are protected by an ICE or PolyPhaser **antenna protector**. These small protectors are mounted directly to the metal grounding plate previously described. Your antenna comes down the wall and connects **first** to this connector. Then you use another short piece of antenna coax cable to connect the outlet side of this connector to your radio.

RADIATION METER

Sources: Dosimeter Corporation Radiation Survey meter: Model 3510 (about $700) or a refurbished government style survey meter model 717 from http://www.radmeters4u.com/

(About $250). Cheap alternate: KFM homebuilt radiation meter kit (about $10) Order from Emergency Essentials (1-800-999-1863)

Because there will be no warning of a nuclear attack before the actual attack and because of the possibility of no news coverage afterward (due to EMP effects), many people will never know they are being exposed to large, fatal doses of nuclear gamma radiation–especially in areas where a military target is not present and no fireball is seen. Even if one is warned sufficiently in advance to seek cover, one would not know how long to stay protected without a radiation meter. Just because others are ignorant and walking around outside after an attack does not mean it is safe. You should mentally calculate how long it would take airborne fallout particles to reach your home from the nearest military installations (all major installations will be hit) if the wind is blowing from that direction. On the day of an occurrence if the wind is blowing from a direction of a nuclear strike, calculate how much time you have to round up your children and friends etc. and get into a sheltered location. Learn to sense how fast the wind is blowing–not just at the surface but by watching the speed or movement of clouds and tall trees. You can then predict how soon potential fallout will arrive. After the initial strike, more strikes may come later, and you will even experience invisible fallout particles from much further away, depending upon the prevailing winds. So be aware of the prevailing high altitude winds and jets streams. The only way to be sure of the presence of fallout is with a meter. If you see physical particles falling from the air, you are in extreme danger, not only of gamma radiation but of beta burns, which occur when certain particles land on you and are not washed off quickly.

The expensive Dosimeter meter, Model 3510 or mid-priced Victoreen 717 are best because they will cover the full range of dosages from high to low, with 3 different scales, and does not require any expertise to use or interpret. Be sure you have at least one extra 9 volt battery for it. Many meters are only designed for low levels of radiation, for workers in nuclear power plants. These types will read "off the scale" almost constantly during a nuclear crisis, giving you no useful information except that the situation is still unsafe. The cheap home built meter is wide-ranging, proven and accurate, but requires some expertise to operate. It also requires fairly dry conditions to give it an initial static charge. This static charge will discharge over time in the presence of radiation. Timing this falling static discharge and comparing it to a built-in chart is the key to its operation. The kit actually has enough parts to build 2 or 3 little meters if you supply additional little cans the size used for tomato sauce.

Whatever the meter you use, you should take hourly readings from inside your shelter to chart how much total radiation you are experiencing. A reading of 100 rems on your meter each hour for 10 hours equates to a total dosage of 1000 rems. Don't let yourself get exposed to that much radiation without piling more solid things above you. In general, a moderate dose spread over a long period of time is better than the same dose received in an hour. Think of gamma radiation as ultra-high speed microscopic bullets that are cutting through your cells injuring nuclei, genetic structures and cell walls. The body can repair some of this if the system is not overwhelmed by too much damage in too short of a time. Radiation dissipates fairly rapidly, and thus it is very critical that you do not run around collecting things for the shelter during the initial radiation period. Get under as much cover as possible, as soon as possible, even if severely uncomfortable. Each succeeding day will be a little safer to venture out, if you have to, to secure food or water, or take care of sanitary needs. But even this is not recommended and speaks for the necessity of having all the necessities of this list prepositioned both to avoid running around just before fallout arrives, collecting things, or worse yet, running around collecting things after fallout arrives.

If directly down wind of a nuclear explosion, you can easily be subjected to radiation in the range of 1000 to 3000 rems per **hour**. Anything in excess of 1000 rems **total** radiation is fatal. So you can see, this is not a danger to be trifled with. For example, the downwind deadly zone (where dosage exceeds 1000 rems) for a 2 megaton weapon, with 15 mph winds is an area 40 miles downwind and 10 miles wide within 18 hours of the explosion. After a week, the deadly zone is 80 miles long and 20 miles wide. On the positive side, most people outside of this range will only receive radiation in the 100-300 rems per day range, depending upon the distance, which gives somewhat more leeway. But long-term illness such as cancer and leukemia are still a major threat. The fatalistic view of, "Well, we're all going to die anyway, so why prepare?" is just not true. In fact, most people will not die, but they may wish they had died, due to the horrible nausea and internal bleeding associated with radiation sickness. Coupled with the probability of little access to medical care (none of our medical facilities or personnel are effectively sheltered) there will be much suffering.

Radiation Effects Summary

The following is a brief synopsis of the biological effects you can expect from certain cumulative doses of radiation:

Below 100 rems cumulative, (rems are the units you read from your radiation meter) there are almost no serious medical problems. From 100 to 200 rems total dosage, the victim will experience some nausea and vomiting on the first day or two. Thereafter, there will be a loss of appetite and general feeling of weakness and apathy. Mild leukopenia (loss of white blood cells) occurs and damages the body's immune system, making it less able to fight illness and the direct damage caused by radiation. The more severe the onset and degree of initial symptoms the longer the recovery, but all will recover in this dosage range.

From 200 to 600 rems, the internal damage to blood and organs is sufficient that hospitalization (if available) will usually be required. Blood transfusions and antibiotics are required for recovery. Hair loss if evident above 300 rems, and internal hemorrhaging occurs frequently above 500 rems. If no hospital facilities are available, which is probable, be prepared to find a nearly sterile recovery area for such people and apply the best herbal and vitamin immunal recovery technology available. A supply of immune enhancing herbs and vitamins is essential, as well as filtered dry air and clean water. Be sure you have plenty of the following health supplements:

- Multi-vitamin pill (do not buy synthesized vitamins, only natural, organic ones)
- Vitamin C with bioflavanoids, rosehips (Vit C is a universal anti-oxidant, anti-viral and anti-bacterial compound) take in large doses (1 gram size)
- Vitamin E (400 IU size), Vitamin A
- Calcium Citrate with Manganese, Zinc, boron and Vitamin D.
- Vitamin D is very essential since you will get no sunlight on your skin.
- B-complex
- Garlic (universal antibiotic) (fresh is best, but store pills)
- Immune enhancing herbs: Echinacea, Pau d'Arco, and Golden Seal
- Kelp tablets and colloidal sea based mineral supplements with iodine.
- Stabilized Oxygen Preparations (Aerobic K07) Purifies water, adds oxygen to blood to purify and remove toxins, and treats bacterial intestinal disorder

Recovery above 500 rems exposure is with guarded optimism at best–and only if you have the ability to treat infection and immunal deficiencies. Death may occur within 1 to 6 weeks.

Above 1000 rems total body exposure, recovery is nearly impossible since the gastrointestinal tract as well as the blood circulatory system is severely damaged. In addition to the former symptoms are added severe diarrhea, fever, and the disturbance of the body's electrolyte balance. Death occurs within 2 to 14 days. Exposure above 5000 rems leads to almost immediate nausea symptoms and a shutdown of the central nervous system within 1 to 48 hours. Cause of death within 1 or 2 days is from respiratory failure and brain edema.

Let me repeat the essential precautions: Make certain that anyone coming into your home or shelter, after fallout particles have started to rain down, is washed down completely, and discards all clothing which may have dust particles imbedded. Check them with a meter to make sure they are not carrying radiation particles into your shelter. Keep extra used clothing (like underwear and loose fitting sweats) for just such an emergency. If you are caught outdoors when particles begin descending, cover your head and mouth with anything suitable to minimize the ingestion of radioactive particles, and run for shelter. Once in your lungs, these particles cannot be removed.

Note on Economization

The instructions which follow will take you step by step through all major facets of construction. Due to financial constraints some of you may not be able to afford to do everything or prepare for every contingency we have outlined. In fact, it is not possible to prepare for everything, literally. Let me suggest some helpful hints on where you can compromise and economize, and when you should not. First, the absolute essentials–do not compromise on these:

Make sure you at least construct some sort of concrete vault room, stock it with at least 50 gallons of water, two weeks of food, some camping utensils, a chemical toilet, a radiation meter, a short wave radio, something to sleep on, some flashlights and batteries, one oil or propane lamp, one military surplus gas mask per person and one filtered inlet pipe. This is the "bare bones" level of protection. You'll have light, food, water, some news of what is going on, and a safe, secure place to wait it out. You may have some discomfort, and you won't have much flexibility or options to maneuver, but you will probably survive almost any two week catastrophe. For longer term emergencies, you'll need to prepare a lot more.

Here are some compromises you can consider:

1. Do the labor yourself. You will save almost half the cost of the Shelter

2. You can economize on the door, by going from a vault door (about $2-4000) to a 14 gauge steel utility door (in metal frame) with or without a ¼" steel plate attached to the front with hardened stove head bolts (rounded heads) that go all the way through the utility door. The steel utility door is less than $500 and the steel plate will cost another $200. Mild steel will resist most intrusions but is not bullet proof. Heat treated 3/8" steel for a door front can be purchased from Heflin Steel in Phoenix, Arizona, for about $900. This plate is very tough and will stop bullets up 7.62 caliber (military rifle types). The detail sheets on "Concealed Door Systems" shows you how this steel plate is installed on the steel door. If you opt only for a steel utility door, make sure you specify a high security deadbolt like "ASSA" or Medico brand. True high security dead bolts are not available at home builder's stores, no matter what it says on the package about "heavy duty" or "commercial grade". If you don't pay close to $100, the deadbolt isn't good enough or pick-proof. But even then, your money spent on a vault room has been strongly compromised by the weak link in the system–the door. At least, you can always add the steel face plate later, when you can afford it.

3. You can do away with the electrical system altogether if you want to. Simply stockpile flashlight batteries for lighting, in combination with some propane or fuel oil lanterns. Make sure you have batteries for the radios as well. Keep them cool to prolong storage life. Remember that having light in a windowless shelter is very important. You can actually survive without it, but not if you get sick and need light to find the right treatment, or if something goes wrong and you need light to fix it. There is also the psychological factors involved in being cold, dark and hungry–which may affect children's ability to handle the emergency (which, in turn, may affect whether or not you have any peace and quiet in the shelter).

4. The next step up from flashlights is to simply install the 12-volt battery bank on a 110 volt trickle charger. Once the electricity goes off, you won't be able to recharge the batteries, but you will probably get at least two weeks of lighting off the battery bank, without recharging. The next step up is to add an inverter/charger. It keeps the batteries at a much more consistent level of charge during non-use periods, and also gives you 110 volt power from your batteries during the emergency. This inverter can also help you run things in your house during lesser emergencies (common, short-term power outages) when the shelter is not needed. The last phase (and most expensive) is to add the solar charging system. The panels will cost you about $400-500 each, even at Abraham Solar's special prices. The charge controller will cost about $50-150. Try to buy at least one panel, and have a spare inside the shelter in case EMP or storms hurt the ones outside. Naturally, you can't replace those panels till radiation is low.

5. You can do away with interior and exterior fire and sound proofing, and go with bare concrete walls. Your vault room is still, **very** fireproof–you just won't be able to stay inside for over an hour in a fire without getting overheated. The structure will stay intact, but it just gets hot, and that heat will become intolerable after an hour or so— unless you have a tunnel exit. But that still is quite a long period, considering that most fire departments will respond to save you before that time (except in war). The trade off, therefore, is only in human survivability inside. Your personal papers and valuables will not be damaged even by the high temperature if kept at least a foot away from the walls, and inside some type of container. Soundproofing is only important if you are hiding from intrusion in a concealed entrance shelter, and do not want anyone to locate you. Even without the fire/sound proofing, a 12" concrete shelter is very sound resistant to low frequency sounds–though not as much to high frequency or impact sounds.

6. In your water storage, you can avoid plumbing costs by simply using static water storage in plastic barrels or old water heating tanks, filled, purified, and capped. You will have to change water every 3-5 years (with Aerobic K07 added) depending on how warm the water gets, but at least you'll have some. But do not economize so much that you do not at least provide some access holes for future water and electrical. These should be small and plugged up temporarily, so remodeling will not be an extensive and difficult endeavor.

7. You can eliminate the concealed entrances, or delay their implementation. If you have a high security door, your room will not be easily breached, even if someone knows where it is.

8. Lastly, you can economize on the amount of equipment and stockpiles you choose to place in the shelter.

But remember, it is most important not to make what I call "irreversible" errors–things that cannot be changed or added without extensive tear-down and rebuilding–such as:

- Undersizing the shelter
- Not allowing for an emergency exit
- Failing to provide for future plumbing, electrical, antennas or ventilation
- Placing it in a compromising or improper location.

Cost Estimate

The following is a rough estimate of costs to build a sample shelter of the size (8' x 16') that we have proposed in this report. This comes to about $15,000 in materials and equipment, for the do-it-your-selfer (year 2008). If contracted, about $30-40,000.

MATERIALS:		
concrete block	$2000	
R-bar	600	
Steel decking	800	
bunk beds	250	
sheet rock	170	
steel studs	200	
insulation	250	
sand, cement, lime	600	
electrical wire	200	
electrical boxes, fixtures	200	
misc plumbing fixtures	500	
cabinets	1000	
interior doors	300	
misc hardware	150	
TOTALS	**$7220**	
EQUIPMENT		
steel door/jamb	800	(Vault door $3800)
water tanks	300	
solar array	1200	
inverter	850	
batteries	500	
dc controls, boxes	600	
EMP equipment	700	
radios, antenna	500	
chemical toilet	40	
radiation meter	250	(700 for Dosimeter)
deadbolt	100	
12 volt fixtures	200	
marine toilet	275	
ventilator fans	120	
security/intercom	1000	
TOTALS	**$7435**	

CHAPTER THREE

HOW TO BUILD YOUR HS SHELTER

STRUCTURAL CONSIDERATIONS
WALL AND CEILING STRUCTURAL ELEMENTS

For ease of modular construction, we will specify the use of 12 inch concrete blocks for free standing walls and 6 inch block against basement walls. When the voids (holes) in the center are reinforced with steel reinforcing rods (R-bar) and filled with cement grout, they are nearly equivalent in strength and radiation shielding to poured concrete. They are however, much more convenient for the do-it-your-selfer to use, and much more conducive to construction inside an existing house.

For purposes of "unibody construction", we will build four new walls even when building this unit next to basement walls. We want this high security room to act as a unit in an earthquake. The worse thing you want is for a ton of ceiling concrete to come down on you because the shifting of the earth made the ceiling come away from the basement wall it was partially resting on. You can use 6" block on the wall next to a basement wall.

As mentioned before, the structure must have no windows and only one conventional-sized door to lessen the security problems associated with multiple entrances and to lessen the need for radiation shielding of too many entrances. All entrances should be concealed from the outside. In any long-term catastrophic emergency, the chances of encountering, crime, and pillaging of homes is very high. In addition it is well documented, historically, that governments intervene to confiscate personal supplies at will, without regards to individual property rights–especially in time of war. For numerous reasons of security and safety there should also be one emergency underground exit leading to a concealed exterior location which cannot be blocked by rubble or debris.

The shelter should provide a minimum **radiation protection factor** (PF) of 32. This effectively cuts one's exposure to gamma radiation to 1/32th of what would be received without protection. This is achieved by providing concrete or masonry walls and ceiling of 12 inch thickness, in an above ground structure. In a basement, the earth provides more than enough shielding for the walls, thus, only 8" thick walls are sufficient (for structural reasons.) A 12" thick, steel reinforced concrete block ceiling will be built over the security room. If cost is not a factor, you may desire to provide thicker walls and ceilings for even greater shielding–but this is not cost effective for most people. The costs of equipping a shelter are considerable and funds must be reserved for this purpose. If you live within 5 miles of a major military base you should make provisions to protect against the effects of the blast itself, as well as the subsequent nuclear radiation—or relocate. This involves expensive blast doors and vents, which is beyond the scope of this paper (and perhaps your finances, as well). I believe it is sufficient in almost all cases to simply increase the amount of steel reinforcement in the ceiling of the shelter. The reinforcing herein specified will allow your vault room to survive direct blast effects up to 2 miles away, if in a basement location, and within 3 miles if above ground. It would most likely survive with some damage at even closer distances, but I recommend you move away if you are living that close to any major military installation. If you must survive in a blast area you are better off purchasing a dedicated burial type Steel Culvert shelter from *Utah Shelter Systems* that come with integral blast valves. The cost is much more and space utilization is diminished.

CEILINGS

While a comprehensive structural plan would depend upon many design factors specific to the size and shape of your shelter, the following reinforcement for a self-supporting ceiling is sufficient for 12 inch thick poured concrete ceiling spans of 10 feet in width or less:

#5 reinforcement bars (about 3/4 inch thick) every 6 inches across the short span, and #4 bars (about 1/2 inch round) every 12 inches in the long direction. The #5 R-bars should be placed about 1-1/2 inches from the bottom of the form. You might wonder why use the thinner bars on the longest span. It is simply because the weight is borne almost entirely by the large bars in the short direction. The long reinforcement is to tie the grid together and keep it from cracking under stresses other than gravitational. The entire ceiling R-bar grid should be tied into the vertical R-bar in the walls (minimum wall reinforcement should be: #4 bars every 12" vertically and horizontally).

For ceilings constructed of **concrete block**, used in this modular design, we will place one #5 R-bar in each void and then fill the voids with grout. This effectively creates a bonded steel and cement beam across the top of your shelter. We will place ladder wire reinforcement at three different places in the ceiling to bond these ceiling beams together horizontally: one in the middle and one in the first mortar joint from the back, and also the first mortar joint from the front. Of course, with 16 gauge steel decking to hold up the concrete block ceiling, you can simple fill the voids and slide the blocks up on the steel without mortar.

WALLS

Walls next to a concrete basement wall can be made from 6 inch concrete block. The walls that are free standing must be of 12 inch concrete block. The base row of blocks will have a groove ground or chipped out in first course in order to lay a continuous length of #4 R-bar. This will form a bond beam at the base for structural rigidity. Each vertical void of each block will have a length of steel #4 R-bar going from floor to ceiling starting from a drilled hole in the concrete floor. Each horizontal layer of mortar will have a continuous length of ladder wire reinforcement. All voids will be filled with mortar as the wall goes up. This will form a rigid cube of masonry and steel that will resist destruction up to Richter 8 on the seismic scale. It will crack but at least it won't come down on you.

Main Door

Additional shielding and security needs to be added to the main entrance door. Because of the need to control access to the shelter (so that undesirable or contaminated people do not enter without your permission), the main door should be a high security steel door. At a minimum you should provide a 14 ga. steel utility door with metal frame/jamb, set into concrete. For added protection, a 1/4 or 3/8" sheet of steel plate can be bolted to the face, which also adds to the protection of any high security dead bolt you use on the door. I recommend the Swedish ASSA brand deadbolt and lock–which is pickproof. For added protection against projectiles you can order from Heflin Steel in Phoenix, Ariz, 3/8 inch tempered steel plate, which is bullet proof (about $700 plus shipping). Make sure you specify one 1/2" hole drilled in each corner of the panel (3" from each edge) plus a hole for the dead bolt. Once the steel is hardened, it is nearly impossible to drill these holes unless you use a torch to preheat the metal and then use a special hardened drill. This plate weighs about 300 lbs, so it is very difficult to handle and mount without help. Unless you are up to the job, I recommend that most people purchase a ready-made vault door from Homeland Security Safe Company (www.homelandsafes.com)---about $1500.

But even this much steel on a door is not much protection from fallout. One should have a stack of concrete blocks (voids filled) next to the door to stack against the inside of the door after everyone is inside the shelter. If you have room in your design, you can even build a shield wall out of blocks, as is illustrated on the very first drawing in the section on "optimal layout". This provides an L shaped enclosure around the door for shielding, thus allowing continued ease of access, without having to move the blocks back and forth.

Foundation and Floor

In new construction, we would set this heavy structure on its own footings. However, in remodeling and additions, we will place this structure on an existing concrete floor, such as the garage floor. Preferably one or two sides of this vault room must coincide with the existing walls, which are over existing footings. In this way the portions of the vault room that are only sitting on the concrete floor (normally only 4" thick) will have minimal bearing impact. This is because the cube is reinforced and very rigid, thus the weight is distributed mostly to the foundation point which offers the most support–which are the footings under three of the walls. The concrete floors themselves will act as partial footings as long as the walls above them are reinforced and rigid.

What about "Stack Block" Construction?

Some have wondered why I do not recommend the new form of block construction where blocks are stacked without mortar and then covered with a fiber-glass reinforced layer on both sides. This can be used if the steel reinforcement I have specified is maintained. However, the fiberglass reinforced coating on the outside is not, in my opinion, sufficiently strong in an earthquake, and will not withstand forced entry with explosions or pneumatic tools. If you add the specified steel reinforcement to this "stacked" construction, it will be slightly more costly than conventional blocks, due to the high cost of the fiberglass coating. It also lacks sufficient mass for radiation shielding.

Step by Step Instructions for Construction

Let me walk you through the construction of a typical vault room. This will be particularly helpful to both the do-it-your-selfer and also for the homeowner who will want to make sure the builder he hires is doing it correctly. Some builders, especially the experienced old timers have a tendency to want to do things either their "own way" or the way they have done them before. I have a great deal of respect for maturity and hands-on building experience. But there is no substitute for keeping an open mind. Don't let your builder disregard the manner and technique I have specified unless he is sure he knows **why** it was designed that way. If he has a better way, fine, but make sure he can explain to you why it is better, and if it is cheaper, make sure it isn't simply an excuse for the builder to get it done easier and faster–at the expense of strength or resistance to threat. If in doubt, feel free to call me for a quick consultation. If you have limited funds, remember, it is always cheaper to pay for advice before than remedy a mistake afterward.

In the following instructions, I have to take somewhat of a compromise approach. I will discuss and describe the step by step procedures, and will only go into actual construction practice in areas that are unfamiliar to the trained craftsman. I don't have the space or time to make this a book on how to do masonry or how to work with steel. I have to assume that you or your builder knows common construction skills.

I will discuss the project as if you a going to install everything we have talked about. If you are going to economize, you will disregard certain portions. As you read these instructions, refer to the working drawings which immediately follow this chapter. In fact, it will probably be helpful to glance through them first so you will be generally familiar with their contents.

STEPS OF CONSTRUCTION:

1. LAYOUT OF BLOCKWORK

Depending upon the size of the vault room you are going to construct, the layout may or may not accommodate a full line of whole blocks. For ease of construction you should design the size of the room to accommodate whole blocks, end to end–especially the back and front walls, and the ceiling. The voids in these blocks (in the front and back walls) must be aligned as they will contain continuous vertical steel reinforcing that will coincide with the ceiling reinforcing. Because of the heavy steel reinforcement, it is not necessary to overlap the joints of the block as is common construction practice. Every block will be stacked directly above the one below. Layout the back wall first, using a chalk line to indicate both the inside and outside wall surfaces. Make a template of the exact outline of a typical block, and trace each block location on the cement floor, allowing for a 1/2 inch mortar joint between each block (necessary for step #2). Notice, that if you are constructing the back wall up against an existing basement wall, you will only need to use 6" wide block on those walls adjacent to the basement walls. Nevertheless, they will still be 16" in length and will line up with the 12"x16" wide blocks you will use on the front wall. When finished with the back wall, determine and mark the number of whole blocks (if possible) that you will use for the side walls, again leaving 1/2 mortar joint between each tracing, including the ends where they contact the front and back chalk lines. Notice that the length from the outside edge of the side walls will correspond to the total length of the front and back walls (see the drawing labeled "plan view").

If you have done this as recommended, you will have no cutting of block to do except for the block on one side of the vault door. The vault door width does not correspond evenly to the three blocks you will leave out in the front wall for the door installation. As indicated in the plan view, there will be a little more than a half block stack along either side of the door. Place the uncut edge toward the door. Do not be tempted to place whole blocks on either side of the door, and make up the difference at the end of the wall. The normal layout of whole blocks will resume after you get above the door, and this layout must also correspond to the entire ceiling layout, so the reinforcement will be continuous.

Whenever you lay out for a vent or access hole (electrical, plumbing, air vent, battery vent), plan on cutting the particular block involved, or leaving a whole block out and filling in later with cuttings left over from the other cut blocks. Do not shift blocks out of alignment to make holes.

2. DRILL R-BAR HOLES

Drill 1/2 inch holes, 4 " deep so the vertical #4 R-bar will be firmly rooted in the concrete floor. If this depth breaks through the floor, you may create a potential channel for ants or termites to infiltrate. If this is a threat in your area, only drill them 3" deep, so the bottom of the hole is closed. Drill these holes centered in each void of each block you have traced on the floor. In the void next to where the door is going to go, drill two holes about 2 inches apart, and close to the edge of the void in the block. These two R-bar elements will vertically rise inside the block all around the vault door for added security. In addition, they will provide reinforcement on either side of the large bolts that will be placed in the edges of the block to secure the vault door in place.

3. INSTALL AND BRACE VAULT DOOR IN PLACE

The preferred way to ensure a solid installation of the vault or metal door is to set it in place and construct a wood brace around it as shown in the **cut-a-way drawing**. Pre-drill the holes for the side and top bolts that will secure the frame to the block wall. Do these at a height to correspond to a grout joint to avoid having to drill out the side wall of a block. If you do not have the door delivered and wish to install it later, simply install a 6" sleeve of 3/4" galvanized pipe in the proper locations where the bolts would normally be installed, and install them later. However, grouting the airspace between the frame of the door and the block wall is easier done with the door in place as the wall is going up.

The reason I have opted to install the vault door in a recessed manner (as shown in the plans), rather than on the outside of the wall, as designed, is to reduce the intrusion of the out-swinging door into the room when open, and to make the outer edge of the frame more inaccessible to intrusion, when closed and locked. It is equally secure only if the air gap between frame and wall is grouted with concrete, giving more support to the 3 bolts on either side.

Since you or your workers will not have access all around the outside of the construction, you will need to do some work from the inside. For this reason, leave the vault door open during construction. Make sure your bracing is sufficient to handle this heavy door in the open position. Once open, place a solid block under it at the open end.

4. LAY BASE COURSE OF BLOCK, ALLOWING FOR VENT OPENINGS

In laying the base course, it is not necessary to grout the block to the cement floor. It will not bind itself well to old concrete–we depend on the R-bar being drilled into the floor to do this. The only reason for using grout on the bottom would be if the floor is rough or uneven and one wishes to seal the gap. If, however, you are building on a garage floor that is slightly sloped (for drainage, as most are), you will want to grout the bottom in a taper sufficiently to level your vault room. Take care as you are building up to leave penetration openings, where appropriate, for electrical, plumbing, and vents. I always leave at least one extra hole just for something I may have left out. It can be sealed up later if not used.

5. INSTALL TEMPORARY DOWEL RODS or HALF LENGTH R-BAR

There is a problem related to the holes in the floor we have drilled for the R-bar rods. If we leave them empty, for ease of laying block, they will surely get filled in or covered over by grout that falls down into the voids during construction. If we put the full length R-bar in now, we have to lift each block up and down over each rod (don't even think about it). If you don't mind paying for a little more R-bar, the most convenient solution is to cut 4 foot lengths and install them now–it is not difficult to lift block up that high. Then when the walls get up to that level, we fill the voids with cement, and while still wet, we install another length of R-bar, making sure they overlap 30" with the lower bars.

Another way, to avoid wasting a lot of R-bar in the splice, is to insert foot-long wood 1/2 dowel rods or sticks in the holes temporarily. Dip them in oil so any grout that gets around them won't adhere. When the walls get up to where you can still just reach the rods, reach in and pull them out, and install the 7 foot full length bars. You will be ready to build a raised working platform by this time, which will make it easy to raise the block over the full length bars.

6. MAKE "V" GROOVE AND INSTALL BASE HORIZONTAL R-BAR

Make this groove on top of the first row of block, on the interior side of the vertical R-bar. It only needs to be grooved down about 1/4 inch so that the 3/4 inch horizontal #4 bar will fit within the grout joint. If you want, you can economize on effort and just make a 3/4 inch wide grout joint. You will not need ladder wire reinforcement on this first course.

7. AT 2ND COURSE, BEGIN LADDER WIRE and DOOR BOLTS OR SLEEVES

Try to locate ladder wire made for 12" wide block. If you cannot, feel free to use 8" ladder wire. Place a row of ladder wire in every course of grout except the first. Make sure an enclosed section of ladder wire goes around or over the R-bar at the corners and over the double R-bar next to the door. Overlap joints 24 inches. Place battery chamber vent openings at this level if your batteries will be within the vault chamber. See detail on battery vault chamber, later in this section.

8. AT HALF WAY HEIGHT, INSTALL VERTICAL R-BAR

There will be a height difference between the vertical R-bar you install in the front wall versus the back. The front R-bar must not exceed the height of the underside of the future concrete ceiling because the ceiling block will be slid onto the supporting ceiling form from front to back between the gap left in the height of the front wall and the existing room ceiling. If the R-bar is sticking up higher than this front wall, one would not be able to slide the ceiling block through this opening and across the platform built to support the ceiling while it cures.

The back wall R-bar, however, must extend up higher than the wall height and have a 30 inch long portion bent over at 90 degrees (bend in direction of the front wall). This is necessary to tie in the ceiling horizontal R-bar with the back wall vertical R-bar. We will tie in the front wall and the ceiling last.

9. FILL VOIDS UP THIS LEVEL Mortar to fill voids should flow slowly, but not be runny or watery. Tamp it down with a piece of R-bar to ensure there are no air pockets

10. INSTALL NEXT SET OF DOOR BOLTS or SLEEVES AT MID LEVEL

This should be about half wall up the height of the door.

11. BUILD PLATFORM FOR NEXT LEVEL OF WORK

You are now ready to build a two foot platform (or whatever height necessary without hitting your head on the ceiling) so that you can have access to build the higher portions of the wall.

12. CONTINUE WALLS, LADDER WIRE

Remember openings for penetrations, where appropriate.

13. AT 2ND MORTAR JOINT FROM TOP, INSTALL TOP DOOR BOLT/SLEEVE

This is the final bolt in the vertical door sides. There will be one on top part of door.

14. FINISH BLOCK WALL TO HEIGHT OF SHELTER INTERIOR CEILING

This should be no closer to the existing room ceiling than 14", which gives you room to construct the 12" thick ceiling, plus the thickness of the steel decking that will support the concrete ceiling during construction. It is preferable not to penetrate the ceiling with a vent, except at the corner as shown--go out toward the rear wall horizontally at the top, leaving a 1" gap between ceiling construction and the room wall for the air to escape upward toward the ceiling gap, as illustrated below.

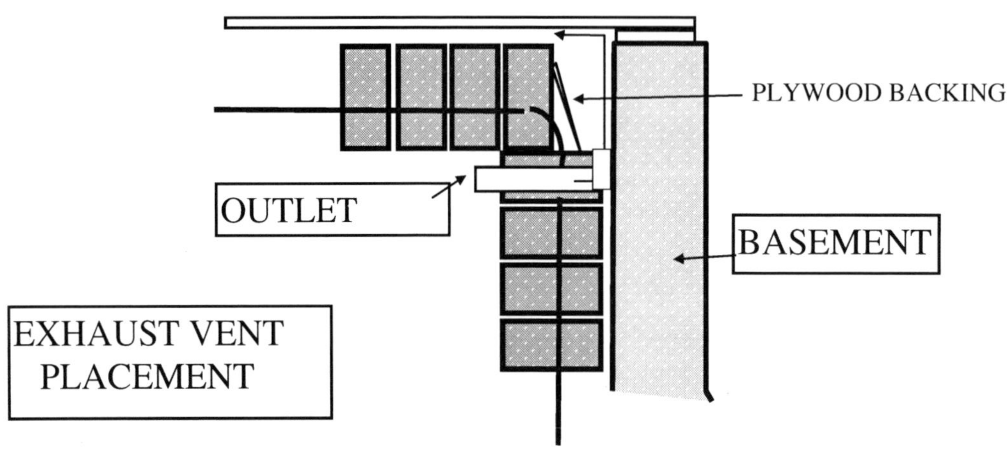

15. BUILD TEMPORARY SUPPORT WALLS AND INSTALL STEEL DECKING

Build a temporary wall out of 2"x4" or use a 6x6 steel I beam to support the middle span. This support may not be necessary if you get heavy 16 or 14 gauge decking that can span 8-10 feet without support. The steel decking should only sit on half the width of the vertical perimeter walls---to allow for ceiling cement to bond around the steel.

With the steel decking in place, you have two ways to do the roof. The first and easy way is to simply slide solid 12" blocks on top of the steel decking until the entire ceiling is covered—no mortar joints. You can make sure it stays together in a quake by simply putting a couple of beads of construction adhesive on the block surface that will go up against the ones already put in place, thus glueing the ceiling blocks together.

The second and harder way is to use hollow 12" block and lay them on their side so that the voids are visible (looking across the short distance of the ceiling). You'll put #4 R-bar in each void and then stuff the void with mortar using a plastic rain gutter as a feed trough. When it hardens, you've created a bond beam out of the blocks—stronger, self supporting and more earthquake proof. The nuclear protection is the same with each.

16. Here's how to do it: Do half the ceiling at a time. First, the R-bar at the rear wall should be bent 90 degrees down over the steel decking; pointing toward the imaginary holes in the block ceiling you will be laying down. Make sure the height of the bent tips is uniform so the holes, or voids in the ceiling blocks will slide over these bent R-bar ends.

Wire a narrow piece of plywood or a short piece of PVC pipe wherever you have an exit air vent coming up through the ceiling as in the foregoing drawing. This will contain the grout that is pushed through the ceiling block voids at that point to make sure the exit air vent won't be stopped up with mortar.

17. LAY HALF OF CEILING BLOCK IN PLACE, PLUS LADDER WIRE

Note that the first course of blocks will not push all the way back to the back wall due to the bent R-bar that emerges from the back vertical wall---that is bent over to engage the ceiling block. That's OK, the mortar will fill in around that empty area when you tamp it through the voids (except where the plywood is to protect the vent). The ladder wire you add after each course binds the bond beams together horizontally when you install the mortar in the voids. The placement of the ceiling blocks is not staggered as when you did the vertical walls. You keep the ceiling blocks perfectly aligned with the previous course so that the voids in each course match exactly.

18. MORTAR THE FIRST HALF OF CEILING VOIDS WHEN COMPLETE. The best method to do this horizontal filling of the voids is to obtain a six foot length of plastic rain gutter, fill about half its length with workable mortar, insert the gutter in the void and

using a push stick with a block at the end matching the shape of the gutter, push the mortar out until it packs into the far end of the void. Repeat as necessary until full.
This takes a little practice, and the use of the pushing board. Don't make the mortar too stiff. You want it to squeeze out anywhere there is a gap of space. The R-bar should lay on the bottom of the void, so the bond beam when set has maximum leverage to withstand deflection. It is easier to fill the voids only half the ceiling width. It becomes very difficult to push mortar horizontally through an empty void for more than four or five feet.

20. FINISH BLOCKS TO SECOND TO LAST COURSE

First, install the last length of ladder wire in this course. Install the last row of ceiling block that will bring the ceiling up to or over the inside edge of the front wall. At this point, we are going to insert into each void a piece of R-bar with a 90 degree bend to tie together the ceiling reinforcement with the front wall reinforcement. The existing vertical and horizontal R-bars should already be within a few inches of each other. But it is necessary to provide this additional bar (as illustrated below), overlapping both existing bars horizontally and vertically so that the wall will stay attached to the ceiling slab under stress or earth movement. Cut these special bent bars so that one part of the bend measures approximately 12 inches and the other end 30". Insert the long end into the ceiling voids and the short end into the front wall voids. Now fill the remaining voids with mortar.

22. FINISH OUTER EDGE

Set up an outside form and pour a finished, square edge out of concrete, as illustrated below: Insert wire ties through plywood and attach to the front wall R-bar to hold form in place. When concrete is set, clip wire ties and remove plywood form. Do this end step for either method—the free block ceiling or the mortared bond beam type ceiling. It will make sure the ceiling stays together as a unit and will also cover up the joint of the raised steel decking (which has a squarish corrugated shape).

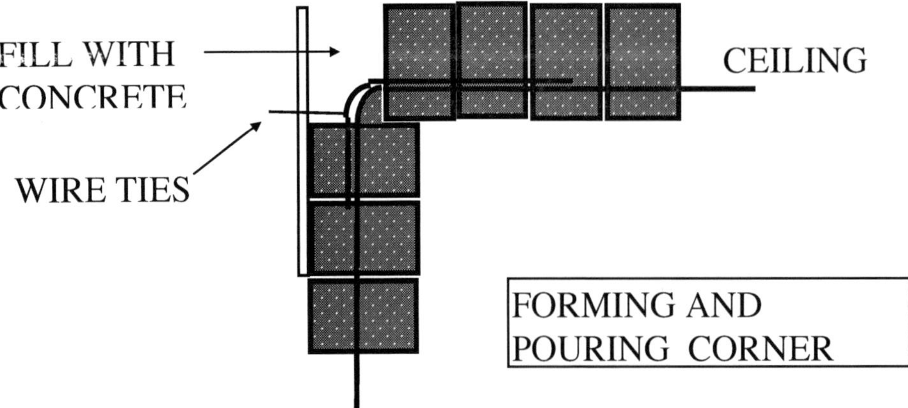

Congratulations: you now have the basic structure complete. After two weeks curing time you can remove the ceiling forms and begin finishing the interior.

Finishing the Interior

As illustrated in the plans, for purposes of fireproofing and sound deadening, we will construct an inner wall and ceiling from steel studs, insulation and 5/8" firecode sheetrock. Working with steel studs is relatively easy. Lay down the base track next to the inner walls, and using a rented "shot driver" (a "gun" which uses .22 blanks to fire concrete nails into the cement) secure the base plate to the cement floor every 24". Nail a similar tract to the ceiling directly overhead, cut the steel studs to length and attach to both upper and lower tracks every 24 inches, according to manufacturer's instructions.

For the ceiling, our spans are small enough that we can support the steel studs from the top of each side wall, using through bolts at either end.

Run electrical and plumbing lines through the pre-cut holes in the studs, to their desired outlet location in the shelter. Make sure you provide electrical outlets on all walls and at least two outlets near the electronic section. Run a separate set of #10 Romex wire to locations where you desire fixed 12 volt lighting and a couple of 12 volt cigarette type outlets (available at RV supply shops). Of course, provide for 110 volt ceiling lights as well, and the appropriate switch boxes near the opening side of the door.

Bring vent pipes through the walls allowing them to intrude into the room at least 2 inches past the steel studs. Insulate walls with R-11 fiberglass batts with foil backing. This backing will go towards the concrete wall in order to repel heat in case of fire. Apply sheetrock only when you are sure you have included everything in the walls that is needed. Apply sheetrock with metal self-tapping screws designed for use with steel studs. Use a screw gun with a special attachment (available at hardware stores) which limits how far in the screw will go before disengaging from the screw gun. Keep all edges and joints tight, as we will only apply mud and tape to the major joints–not over the screws. We want to be able to take down a piece of sheet rock if needed–easy to do with screws.

Exterior Finish

Use the same technique to form a wall outside the shelter. It is permissible to use a wood stud wall, if you desire, on this side. If these few studs eventually burn in a fire, they will not appreciably affect the temperature inside the shelter. But it is important not to use any flammables on the inside wall–especially construction adhesives or foam insulation which will give off toxic fumes when heated to high temperatures. Lay at least one layer of 5/8 inch type X sheetrock on the top of the vault room to ward off the direct impact of burning ceilings above the shelter–it keeps the concrete from excessive heat stress. If you have room between the old ceiling and the new shelter roof to lay down some steel studs (on their flat side) this is an effective way to gain an air space between the two layers of protective sheetrock and the cement below, to help keep it cooler in a raging fire.

Concealed Entrance Construction

This should be done by the owner himself, or by someone absolutely trustworthy. Finish carpentry skills are required to make certain joints look good, but other than this it is not difficult to construct. The designs in the plan section detail two basic types of concealed door entries–a fixed cabinet with a sliding back, and a cabinet which swings out as a unit. The swinging cabinet is more difficult to construct, but is far more effective against discovery because the hinges are completely invisible, it leaves no drag marks on the ground as it opens, and one is capable of loading up the interior shelves so that it looks fully used. The sliding back cabinet only has hanging clothes to disguise its use. The back is not completely rigid so detection is possible to the careful investigator. But it is much easier to construct and use. This sliding design is enhanced by providing moveable wood pieces to go across the back (from inside the vault) which gives it more rigidity against probing. Additionally, once inside the vault room one can screw the back into place so that it physically cannot be slid open from the outside. The same can be done for the swinging cabinet. It should be capable of being secured from the inside of the vault room so that would be intruders cannot open it even if the hidden latch pins are discovered.

Construction of the Battery Vent Chamber

This chamber will also serve as an elevated floor for the water tanks, allowing us to have some gravity flow from the tanks and provide a secure place for the batteries to charge and vent, without endangering the occupants. Lead acid batteries give off hydrogen when charging, which is explosive, in high concentrations. However it doesn't produce a lot of gas, and it is easily dissipated in a large room. It is only a problem in a small confined area or near to the batteries themselves when gassing (in combination with an electrical spark). It isn't going to blow the house up, or even the shelter, but it does present a fire hazard under certain conditions.

So, the first rule is not to put any electronic components into the battery compartment with the batteries–keep them separate. Mount the inverter and the charge controller right outside the cabinet, on a nearby wall.

To store eight 6-volt golf cart batteries, we need a chamber 36 inches wide, 20 inches deep and 12 inches high (interior dimensions). In order to accommodate the weight of two 50 gallon water tanks on top, we will construct a bearing top out of 3/4 inch plywood (marine or outdoor type) and four 2"x4" supports underneath, as illustrated below. This will be supported by short plywood-backed 2"x4" walls on either side, and a 1/2 inch plywood back. All plywood should be attached with construction adhesive and screws to form an airtight and rigid structural box. Holes are cut to correspond to a high vent and a low vent which you should also provide in the vault wall structure as you build up the walls. It is important that one vent be high and the other low, so that a slight circulatory current is set up inside the box. Seal the joint between the pipes that you install and the plywood with caulk so they won't leak. Place mortar around the pipes where they exit the masonry block wall. Make an appropriate hole in the side of the compartment for electrical connections. Once the wiring is through and connected, one can seal it up also. Finally, make a front cover, from 1/4 or 1/2 inch plywood and screw it onto the front. Use thin foam door seal material to provide an airtight seal all around. The bottom is not important to seal, as long as it makes good contact with the floor. We don't want to construct any attachment bar across the bottom so that the heavy batteries can be slid in and out as needed (which will not be very often).

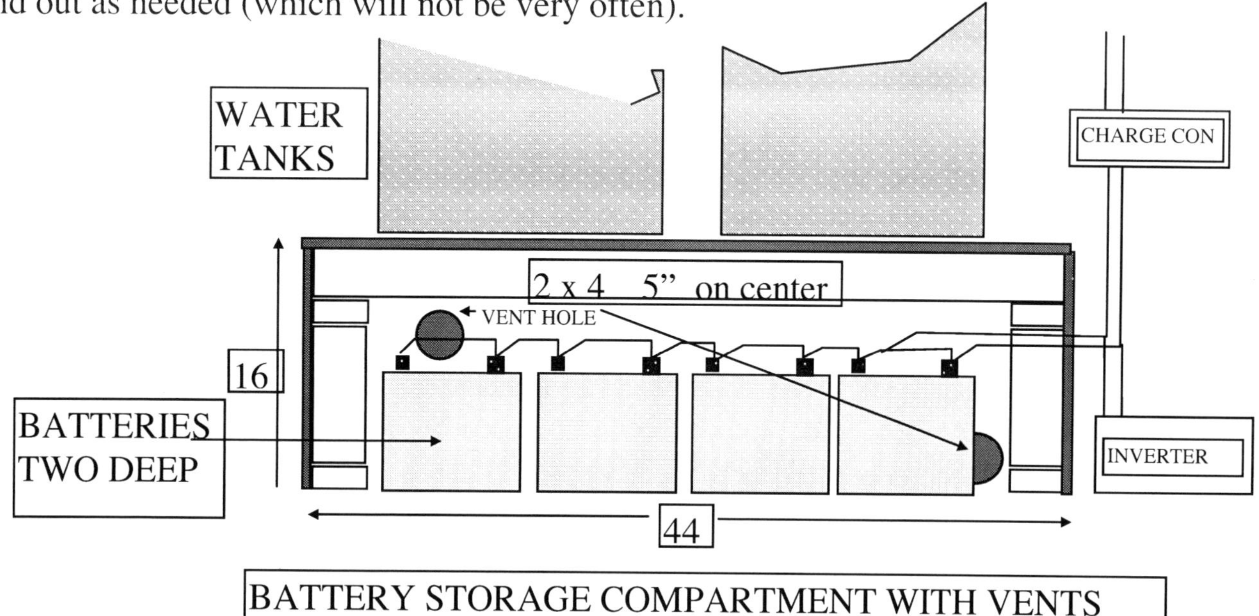

ELECTRICAL SYSTEM SCHEMATIC

The electrical system is composed of the following:

- (4) 75 watt Photovoltaic Modules (producing approx. 3 amps)
- (1) #52-600 fused disconnect for the battery bank and solar array
- (1) Sun Selector NDR-30-12v-cd-EMP charge controller
- (1) #53-075 AEE DC LOAD CENTER
- (1) Trace 812 SB INVERTER w/ Battery charger
- (8) 6-volt Deep Cycle Storage Batteries (wired together for 12 volts)

All of this equipment, except batteries, is available at special prices (10% over wholesale) for purchasers of this book, from Abraham Solar Equipment. (1-800-222-7242)

Provide (2) stranded copper cables (size #4 if less than 50 feet, otherwise go to a #2 cable) from the south side location where your solar collectors are going to be located, into the vault room. The most secure location is on a portion of the roof that is south facing. Placing them at an angle on the ground may be more convenient, but they are less secure there from vandalism.

The positive output from the solar array is connected to one pole of the double disconnect switch, and the battery positive lead is connected to the other (refer to diagram which follows). This allows the disconnect to simultaneously disconnect power from both the battery bank and the solar panels, and also provides automatic fuse protection.

The negative lead from the disconnect switch and the positive lead from the solar array (after passing through the disconnect switch) are then connected to the positive and negative input terminals on the charge controller. Both the disconnect and the charge controller should be mounted on the wall near the battery compartment.

The other positive lead (connected to the battery through the disconnect) is attached to the positive output terminal of the DC load center and then on to the positive output of the charge controller (that says "to battery"). This provides the charging current to the battery from the solar array (via the DC load center). Your 12 volt lights and cigarette lighter type receptacles are attached to the individual output poles on the DC load center.

The DC load center allows individual loads from the battery to be fuse protected and also contains analog meters to indicated battery voltage and charging current as well as discharge current when batteries are being used. This metering is important to help you monitor the status of your batteries.

The positive lead of the inverter is attached through a separate 60 amp fuse block, and the negative lead is attached directly to the battery ground. Make sure you color code your wires leading to the inverter (red for positive, black for neg) so you do not inadvertently connect positive to negative–which will ruin the inverter. Now plug in your inverter and it will keep the batteries perfectly charged as long as there is 110 volt power. Your solar collectors will provide backup charging, and will be diverted to water heating when not charging (if you have a 12 volt water heating coil installed in one of the tanks on top of the battery compartment).

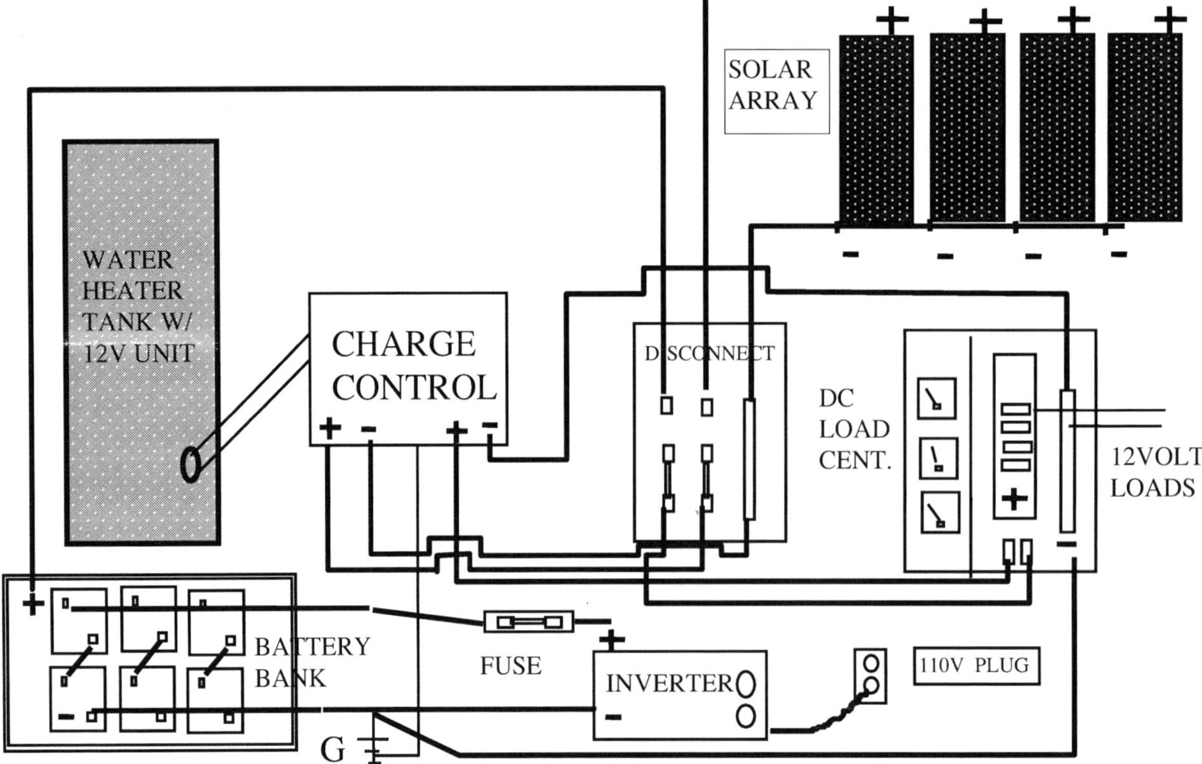

GROUND SYSTEM

A new ground rod should be installed inside the shelter. Drill a 3/4 inch hole in the concrete floor near the counter where you will have most of your electronic equipment. Let a hose dribble water down the hole for a couple of days to thoroughly saturate the ground. Then pour a couple of gallons of water mixed with Epsom salts (1 cup). This provides a much improved electrical contact with the grounding rod. Now drive into the hole a six foot copper ground rod, and leave about 4 inches sticking out of the hole. All ground wires from equipment will terminate here. The 3/4 inch hole is oversized to allow you to pour water down the hole 2 or 3 times a year to keep it moist. Always make sure you do this before the thunderstorm season each year.

The Sun Selector charge controller comes with built-in EMP protection, but for it to be effective; you must establish a ground connection from the "B-" terminal to ground. Do not ground the "PV-" terminal coming from the solar array to any other ground, or it will interfere with the Controller's charge detection circuitry.

The following drawing depicts how to construct an equipment grounding plate for EMP protection and how to connect it to the ground rod:

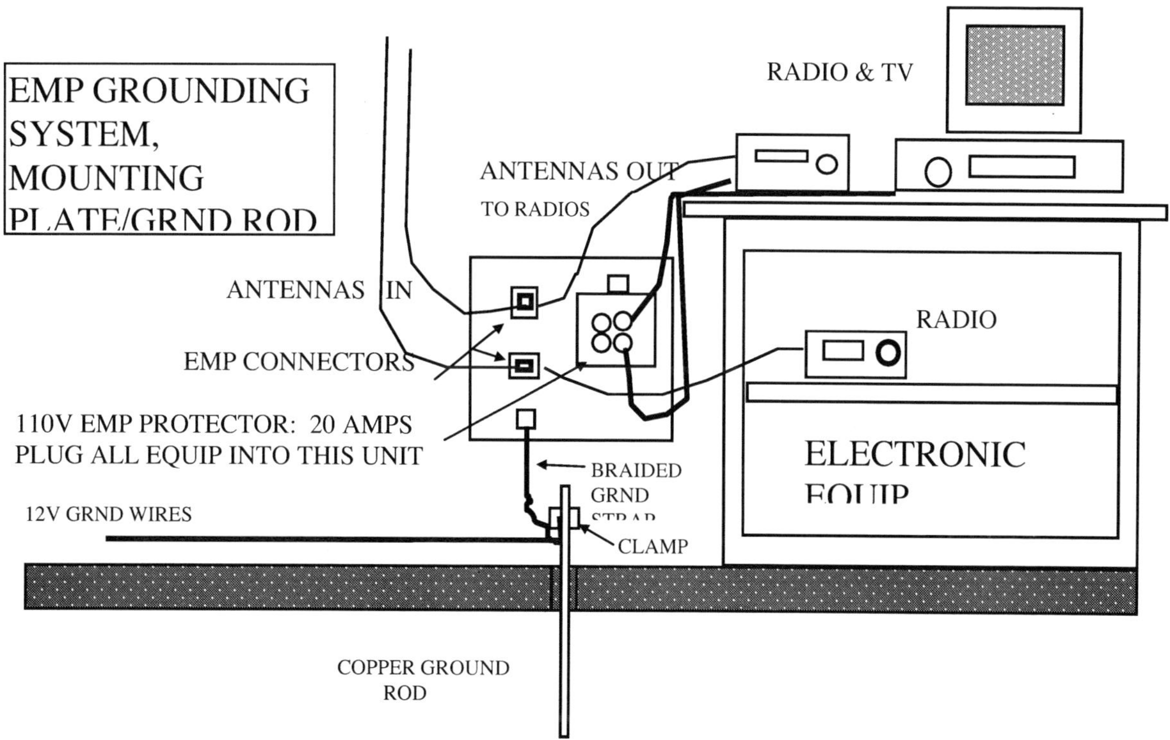

CHAPTER FOUR

How to Fortify a Closet

INTRODUCTION:

There are many reasons why you may want to fortify or "harden" a closet.

1. You may **not have the money** to implement a full-scale HS Shelter with all its specialty equipment, and may want to implement some interim security measures until you can afford the more complete option.
2. You may **not be able to fit** an HS Shelter into your existing home, but want as much security as you can fit into your present situation. Perhaps you are planning on upgrading later to a new custom residence, but want security now.
3. **You may want BOTH**. Your HS Shelter may be some distance away from your Master Bedroom, and you may want to harden the wardrobe closet of your bedroom in order to have a closer, semi-secure room in case you have no easy way of getting from your Master Bedroom to your security room, unobserved.

The third option brings up an important issue--how to achieve immediate security when the threat of intrusion is at your bedroom door. You should, of course, have a solid core door with a locking doorknob on all sleeping rooms (except perhaps for the rooms of very young children). Once an intruder enters your home at night, this locked door to your sleeping chambers becomes a second and very critical line of defense--to give you the precious time you need to telephone for help and secure a suitable defensive weapon to protect yourself

The third line of defense would be the hardened or fortified closet. This option is not only important as a secure room to give yourself additional time and security but to serve as a semi-secure storage for valuables that you may need to access fairly often, where you don't want the hassle of getting into a true vault room each time you want to use them or put them away. Additionally, the secure, hardened closet would considerably delay the time it would take a burglar to get at them in a break-in. In conjunction with almost any sort of burglar alarm, these valuables would at least be safe from a quick "enter, grab and run" attack on your house while you were gone.

Naturally, for longer absences or when you did not have an alarm system that triggers an automatic response from a 24 hour alarm central station, you would want to use a true vault room previous described in this report.

DESIGN AND LAYOUT CONSIDERATIONS:

The optimal candidate for a fortified closet is the typical Master Bedroom walk-in wardrobe closet. It is usually at least six ft. by eight ft. in size and can accommodate a fair amount of extra storage. Unfortunately, many older homes have Master Bedrooms with closets built into the surrounding walls, which utilize bi-fold or sliding doors to cover the contents. These latter types of doors are not true doors, but mere shields and thus are totally unsuitable for security. If you have this type of side-wall closets, you will have to look at two other alternatives to a fortified closet.

1. Build a closet room, if you have enough space in the bedroom, or
2. Select another closet room in the house to harden.

The second option is rarely optimal if it is in a hall way or in another person's bedroom. The hall closet doesn't leave you any privacy getting in or out of the room, and the closet in someone else's bedroom keeps you from having access to it directly from your own bedroom. An office or library with a closet would, however, offer both privacy and good access. If adjoining your Master Bedroom, it may be feasible to add a door linking the two rooms.

In figures 1 and 2 on the following page, I detail two common closet layouts. Most Master Bedrooms with a walk-in closet also have access to a Master Bath. Furthermore, the closet is usually adjacent to the bath. I introduce the bath idea only because it is going to cause some complications in the remodeling process of hardening the closet--which we will have to deal with in some detail. Both floor plans are of the same basic layout. Your home will undoubtedly differ, but most of the principles used in making the conversion will be applicable.

Figure 1 has a normal 8 ft. by 8 ft. closet. Figure 2 has a 10 ft by 8 ft closet. The larger closet in figure 2 is sufficient to implement a double hardening scheme--the walling off of the rear portion to make a secret second compartment for a higher level of security. In the first case, the entire closet is fortified. In the second, either the whole room or the smaller secret portion can be hardened, or both. Let's look at some of the reasons for the apparent redundancy.

1. In Figure 2, we can install a stronger metal door at the closet entrance and paint it to look completely conventional. It will have a locking knob, which allows you to enter and have complete privacy as you open the concealed entrance to the next chamber. Any time you use a concealed or secret entrance to a vault room, it needs to be inside some other room so that you keep prying eyes from observing how you get into the secret room.

2. It is more difficult for thieves to find concealed entrances if such secret doors are located inside a room the intruder already views as secure or secret. It is a bit of the old

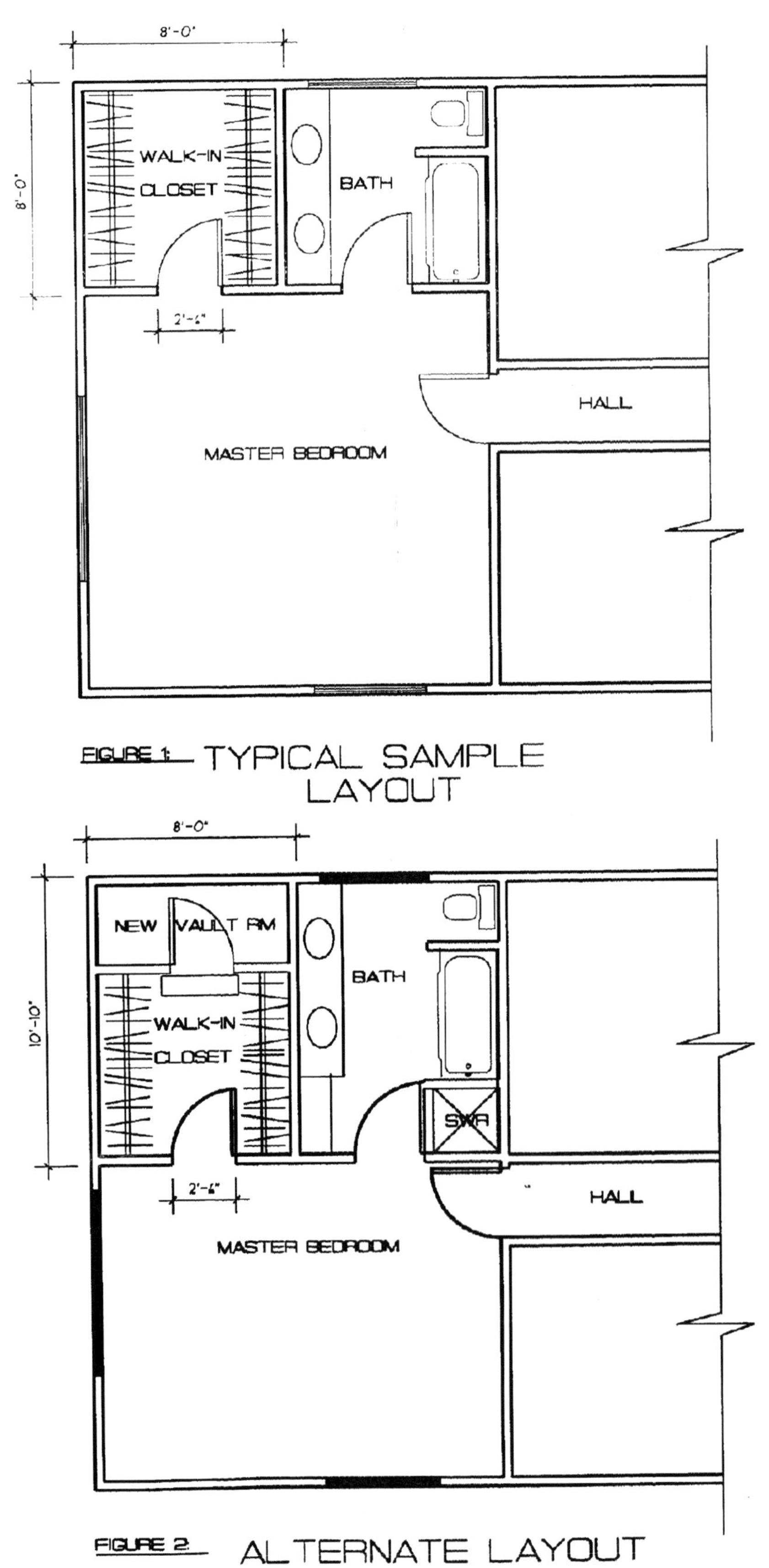

FIGURE 1: TYPICAL SAMPLE LAYOUT

FIGURE 2: ALTERNATE LAYOUT

psychological game of letting the thief feel satisfied that "he has found it." Naturally, to induce him further, one has to have some fake jewels or other "less valuable" items in the first closet for him to steal.

As a general rule, we always try to design into any secure room a second exit for emergency escape. The reasons are not always clear. Let's suppose you have had to go inside your secure closet to get away from a determined intruder--which is now vigorously trying to break down the door. With sufficient force, tools, and time, let us suppose that you fear he may break through. Now it's nice to have a way out--unobserved. As in the HS Shelter, there are also reasons for sometimes wanting to get into your own house unobserved--which these secret access doors allow. These rooms will also provide an emergency escape route in case of fire or toxic smoke and fumes.

Ideally, it is desirable to drop down into a lower room near to your HS Shelter so you can gain access to it quickly, without having to transit the house halls and stairways as you normally would. A crawl space under your house can be a very suitable exit route, depending upon how the crawl space exits the house itself. In designs where the crawl space exits from the house on an exposed outside wall, you may have to build a small attached closet or shed to conceal its use as an exit and to keep others from gaining access to your crawl space via that entrance.

If you must go upwards for an escape route, hopefully you will have a room situated directly above where you can come up into another closet or somewhere near a wall so that the carpeting can conceal the trap door. It is even better when you can access the attic space directly where the escape trap can be concealed by attic insulation. Later on, in figure 6, I detail for you the construction of both the attic and crawl space exits.

DIFFERENT LEVELS OF SECURITY CONSTRUCTION:

While we could construct a whole new closet built to the specifications of the HS Shelter that would be somewhat contrary to the purposes of this cheaper alternative. In the first place, we would need a cement foundation to build upon for a masonry vault room. Most bedrooms built with wood construction do not have this. So we will content ourselves with a hardening technique that utilizes the wood framing of the house.

STRONGER WALLS

The wood framing, usually made of 2" x 4" lumber, 16" on center vertically, is fairly strong and resilient. It is the 1/2" sheetrock board nailed to the wooden studs that is the weakest link. So, in order to increase the intrusion resistance of the walls in this closet, we are going to have to substitute at least 3/4" plywood for the sheetrock (gypsum board). You can do this to both sides of the walls or only one. Doing both is better, naturally, but that's where we run into problems with the walls. Part of the closet will surely be on an outside wall and another wall may face the bath. In both these cases, it may be impossible or too costly to rip out the sheetrock or siding on the other side of the wall. So we may opt to install plywood only on one side on certain walls.

Now, you say, "even plywood isn't going to keep out an intruder with a chain saw." This is very true, and occasionally we find some rural homes that are broken into with the help of a chain saw. We don't see it in the cities much because it makes a lot of noise. But I have an effective way of deterring this kind of intrusion technique. Once we have strengthened both sides of the wall with plywood, we can fill them with packed **3/4" or larger gravel** which does two things. 1, it promises to ruin any chain saw blade in a matter of seconds, and 2, the walls become bullet proof without the cost of solid masonry. We have to use medium sized crushed rock gravel between ½ and ¼ " inch material to absorb the impact. Smaller sizes or smooth pea gravel tends to separate like sand. In fact, the gravel wall solution is a superior bullet proofing to some masonry block, because the gravel gives way sufficiently upon impact to absorb the impact of the bullets, whereas with masonry, enough concentrated fire can chip right through a wall by shattering the rigid block--especially if the voids are not filled and if reinforcing-bars are not used.

STRONGER DOORS

Next come the doors. Hollow core doors are so weak that they can be broken down by any normal sized man even if the door latch is locked. At a minimum we would replace it with a **solid core** door. These are doors that are not hollow, but that are filled with pressed wood fibers or solid hardwood. The latter is best, but more expensive. For an even higher level of security, we could go for a new **metal utility door**, mounted in a metal door jamb, which I will discuss shortly. On top of either the solid wood door or the metal utility door you can add a layer of solid steel plate for real impact resistance. 3/8" mild steel that has been surface hardened will also be bullet proof. But you must use **ball bearing hinges** to bear the weight.

DOOR JAMBS AND LATCHES

Now the next weakest point comes to the forefront--the door jambs. Most door jamb material (the 3/4" by 6" wood surrounding the door, which is nailed to the wall studs) is of pine, is very soft, and splits easily. If we use a solid core door, and stay with a wood jamb, we must replace the screws in the strike plate (where the door latch engages the door jamb, to lock the door closed). Even though your present strike is metal, it usually is only secured with small 3/4" screws. We will take these out and replace the strike with a box type door strike and 3" screws--long enough to penetrate into the actual wood studs on the other side of the door jamb. The box type door strike differs from the normal strike plate in that it has a box of metal where most strikes only have a hole, into which the door latch protrudes. The box type strike keeps the metal from buckling under the pressure of forced entry.

If you opt for the metal utility door, get one with a **metal door jamb**. There are lots of varieties of metal jambs on the marked. Some are no more than flimsy metal pieces you nail over the wood. But the strongest are the type that are one solid piece of formed metal, that wrap around the opening in the wall, and which connect at the top joints with interlocking tabs. They have less flexibility in installation than the adjustable types, and the width of the preformed jamb must match the thickness of your new wall--which will depend on how much plywood and new sheetrock you put on those 2 x 4 studs. More on that later. Of course the metal jamb is only as strong as the number and size of screws you use to attach it to the wooden studs. Use the biggest ones that will fit in the holes, and makes sure they are at least 2" long.

THE LOCKS

Now that the walls, doors and jambs are beefed up, we need a stronger door knob and lock. Several lock makers make a very heavy duty door knob (like Schlage)--one that can't easily be knocked off with a hammer. Get one with a high security lock cylinder--that means that it uses a non standard key that can't be easily picked. Ask your local locksmith what he can get for you. In addition, you will want to install a pick-proof high security dead bolt, (such as ASSA makes). If you install a steel plate over the door, make sure the holes are cut precisely to match the door knob and dead bolt. When tightly fitted, this steel plate helps secure the locks in place and makes them almost impossible to break off with a hammer. Remember too, that dead bolts plus the door latch give you two points of resistance to forced entry rather than one heavy duty one--which makes it less likely someone big and strong is going to be able to shoulder-in the door.

OPTIONAL DOOR BRACES

As a final security against forced entry, I recommend you install on the inside some old fashioned pioneer type door braces--like a 2 x 4 that goes across the door in two places, held in place by U shaped brackets attached to the door jambs with lag bolts. Place one cross brace about 1/3 down from the top of the door and one at the same distance from the bottom of the door. These braces will give you real peace of mind if you are inside and someone is trying to break in either the upper or lower half of the door.

THE CEILING:

A layer of 3/4" plywood also needs to be placed on the ceiling as well to keep out would be intrusions from the attic or second story

To summarize, let me outline three different levels of security, even though you can mix and match different aspects of each, if you like:

LEVEL ONE (the cheapest and easiest): remove inside sheetrock only and replace with 3/4" plywood on both walls and ceiling. Add new 1/2" sheetrock on inside and finish to match original closet condition. Add solid core door, new beefed up strike, new heavy duty door know and dead bolt, and door braces.

LEVEL TWO: remove wall material on both sides where feasible (except exterior siding--which is usually strong enough to resist entry) and install plywood on both sides, then new finish material to match existing condition. Add metal utility door, with heavy duty knob and locks plus metal door jamb.

LEVEL THREE: Same as level two but with added packed 1/2" gravel in wall cavities for intrusion and bullet proofing. Also add hardened steel plate to door front.

OTHER ESSENTIALS FOR ALL LEVELS:

All fortified closets should have a telephone jack install for communication, and/or the capability of calling out with a cellular telephone. If the gravel option inhibits reception, feed an external cellular antenna into the attic space. All closets should also have an emergency escape exit which is concealed. You should have some form of defensive weaponry inside this closet as well--preferably a hand gun or pepper spray.

CONSTRUCTION TIPS

WALLS

There are several decisions you will have to make concerning the walls. The major one involves removing the sheetrock so that you can install the stronger plywood panels. First remove any carpeting on the floor so it will not be damaged in the remodeling. Within the closet itself, you will usually have to remove the shelves and wood supports that are nailed through the sheetrock. To do this with minimal damage to the wood, first remove the top shelf. Then find the studs the wood supports are attached to. Use a flat pry bar between the wood and the sheetrock at this point (if you do it elsewhere it will break through the sheetrock, and deny you any leverage). Now remove the sheetrock itself. If you pull hard after punching a fist sized hole in several locations, the board should pull away easily.

The outside walls are more problematic, especially if you have a bathroom on one side. Even that isn't an insurmountable problem unless you happen to have a tub or shower on that wall, or some fancy wallcovering. In that case, you may not want to remove the wall board. Instead, we will use another technique to strengthen the inner side of the wall board. But first, let's go over the details of applying the plywood to walls that can be accessed. Refer to figure 3 on the following page for this discussion.

In figure 3, we see a horizontal cross section and plan view of the closet, with a small added vault room in the rear. The 2 x 4 studs in the old walls were pre-existing, except for where we have added the new partition wall for the inner secure area. Where this new wall meets the old wall we have added an extra vertical 2 x 4 stud on each side, so we have something to nail the new plywood and sheetrock to. Before installing the new plywood walls, pull off any electrical boxes from the studs on walls or ceiling and renail the boxes 3/4 of an inch further out into the room. This way, you will still be able to attach your electrical fixtures through the added wall material. If the screws don't reach, you can buy longer ones at any lighting or hardware store. Now, let's put in some gravel:

INSTALLING GRAVEL:

First, when all the framing is done, put up the plywood along the lower 4 feet of each side of the wall--by laying the long side of the plywood against the floor. Naturally, you will have to pre-measure and cut out for any electrical boxes on the walls and ceiling. Don't forget to install the new telephone lines before putting on the plywood. Attach the plywood with construction adhesive and then screw it to the wall with 1-1/2 inch grabber screws. These are much more secure than nails. We want a wall that will not separate from the studs under hammering or impact. Pour in the gravel now up to the half-way point. Next install the upper half of plywood, but before doing so, cut off the top 4 inches. Pouring in the gravel up at the top is more difficult. Use a dustpan as a shallow scoop to do the filling. When the cavities are full, pound on the walls with a hammer to settle the gravel, then fill again. Finally, install the 4 inch strips you cut off before, trimming as needed..

Now, let's backtrack to our bath wall. Installing gravel when the bathroom side of the wall is not reinforced with plywood may cause the sheetrock wallboard to break away from its nails. In an earthquake, or with hard tamping of the gravel fill, sheetrock will collapse. Figure 6 shows how to reinforce this wallboard from the inside of the closet. We use some 1/2 inch plywood and cut it lengthwise into strips just wide enough to fit into the cavity between the studs-. Cut some 1 inch wide sheetmetal straps long enough so that when they are tacked on the back of this plywood, both ends extend out to the sides about 3". Nail these on the back of the plywood board every foot from bottom to top. Push the board back into the cavity with the straps between the plywood and the old wallboard. Now set a nail into each end of the straps that are now pressed up against the studs on either side. This will keep the gravel from transferring its weight to the sheetrock. It's a little extra work, but it sure is easier than tearing out bathroom walls and fixtures and trying to put them back.

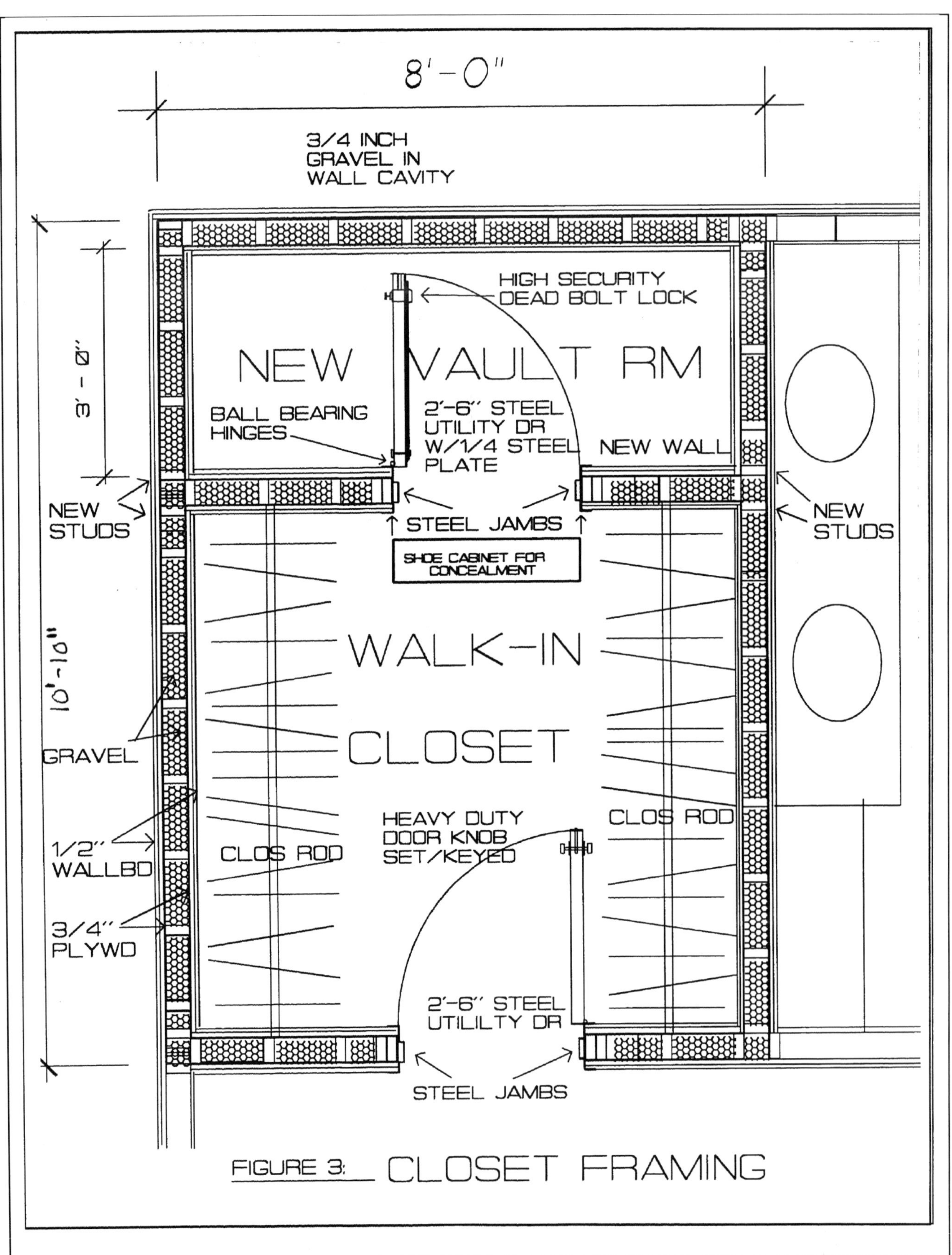

FIGURE 3: CLOSET FRAMING

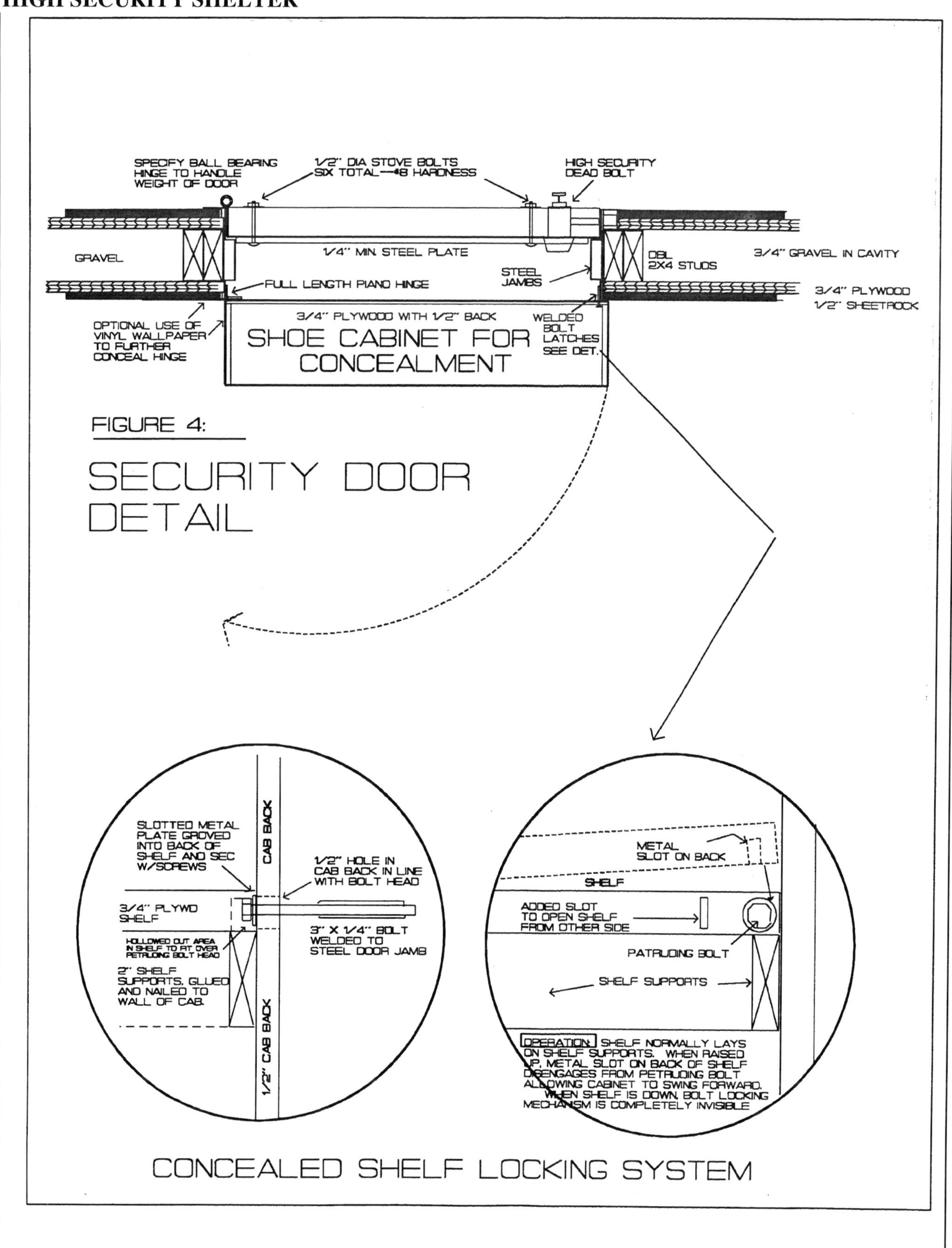
SPECIFY BALL BEARING HINGE TO HANDLE WEIGHT OF DOOR
1/2" DIA STOVE BOLTS SIX TOTAL—#8 HARDNESS
HIGH SECURITY DEAD BOLT
GRAVEL
1/4" MIN. STEEL PLATE
DBL 2X4 STUDS
3/4" GRAVEL IN CAVITY
STEEL JAMBS
FULL LENGTH PIANO HINGE
3/4" PLYWOOD
1/2" SHEETROCK
OPTIONAL USE OF VINYL WALLPAPER TO FURTHER CONCEAL HINGE
3/4" PLYWOOD WITH 1/2" BACK
SHOE CABINET FOR CONCEALMENT
WELDED BOLT LATCHES SEE DET.
FIGURE 4:
SECURITY DOOR DETAIL
SLOTTED METAL PLATE GROVED INTO BACK OF SHELF AND SEC W/SCREWS
CAB BACK
1/2" HOLE IN CAB BACK IN LINE WITH BOLT HEAD
3/4" PLYWD SHELF
HOLLOWED OUT AREA IN SHELF TO FIT OVER PETRUDING BOLT HEAD
3" X 1/4" BOLT WELDED TO STEEL DOOR JAMB
2" SHELF SUPPORTS, GLUED AND NAILED TO WALL OF CAB.
1/2" CAB BACK
METAL SLOT ON BACK
SHELF
ADDED SLOT TO OPEN SHELF FROM OTHER SIDE
PATRUDING BOLT
SHELF SUPPORTS
OPERATION: SHELF NORMALLY LAYS ON SHELF SUPPORTS. WHEN RAISED UP, METAL SLOT ON BACK OF SHELF DISENGAGES FROM PETRUDING BOLT ALLOWING CABINET TO SWING FORWARD. WHEN SHELF IS DOWN, BOLT LOCKING MECHANISM IS COMPLETELY INVISIBLE
CONCEALED SHELF LOCKING SYSTEM

CEILING

Take down the electric lighting fixture on the ceiling, remove the sheetrock and apply 3/4 plywood just like you did on the walls. Lower the electric box 3/4 inch. If you are installing your escape trap door in the ceiling, install support bracing as per figure 6 on the following page before screwing and gluing the plywood to the rafters. Gravel will be installed on top of this plywood from the attic. Do not fill the cavity spaces more than 3 inches deep with gravel to keep the weight down. Then from the attic, nail rabbit wire over the gravel. This is to make it difficult for anyone to remove the gravel and get access to the plywood roof, if they should discover it. Cut the wire wide enough so that it can be nailed to the part of the rafters that extend above the gravel. Note that in figure 6, we have placed a piece of 1/2 inch plywood above the trap door and then a light layer of grave so as to disguise the location of the trap entrance. The wire over this area should be nailed with very small nails that can be easily pulled out by pushing on the wire from below. Once all the wire is in place, put attic insulation back over the top so that nothing shows.

VENTILATION:

Just in case you ever have to spend a night in your secure closet, you will want some ventilation to avoid suffocation. One of the easiest ways is to install a bathroom fan in the ceiling and duct the exhaust to the attic, or even another room upstairs. If you can't get electricity to this closet, a simple 3" pipe going to the attic will allow you to draw air with your own lungs. Make sure you put a screened covering on the attic side of the pipe, so mice cannot enter your secure room. You can add a filter system if you wish.

DOORS:

Figure 4 on the previous page covers the installation of new doors. The most difficult thing to deal with will be the added wall thickness. A normal 2 x 4 wall with 1/2 inch wallboard on either side will be 4-1/2 inches thick. So the existing door jamb wouldn't be any good even if you wanted to keep it in place. If your closet walls are built of 2 x 4 studs (which are 3-1/2 inches thick) and you have both sides covered with 3/4 inch plywood plus two sides of 1/2 inch wallboard, your total wall thickness at the door jamb will be 7 inches. The closest standard door jamb width is 6-1/2, which is too narrow. If you go with a wood jamb you can buy a wider jamb and have it cut down. If you use metal jambs, you can either go with the adjustable jambs or the preformed 7 inch jambs. If you can only get the 8 inch metal jambs, just fill in the inside portion with wood, where it won't show. Note that the doors should open inward into the closet so that the hinges are not exposed for the intruder to tamper with. Be sure and get 14 or 16 gauge doors--usually an item only sold by commercial door outfits. Look at the side edge of the door. If you see any wood, it is not the right type. All sides and edges should be of metal.

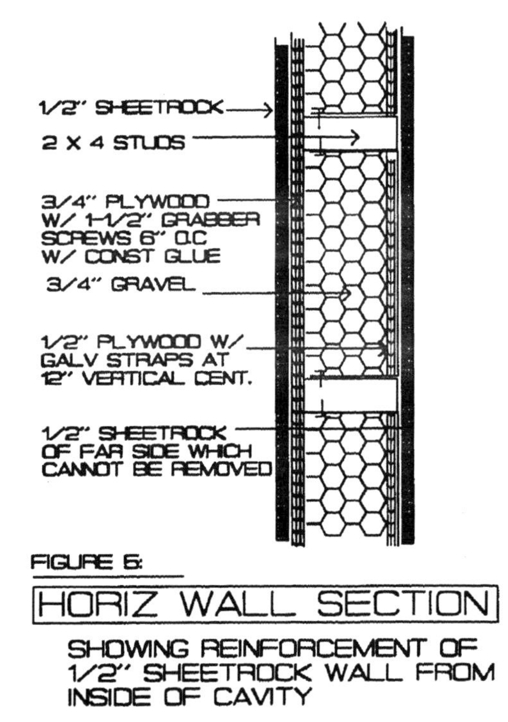

FIGURE 6:

HORIZ WALL SECTION

SHOWING REINFORCEMENT OF 1/2" SHEETROCK WALL FROM INSIDE OF CAVITY

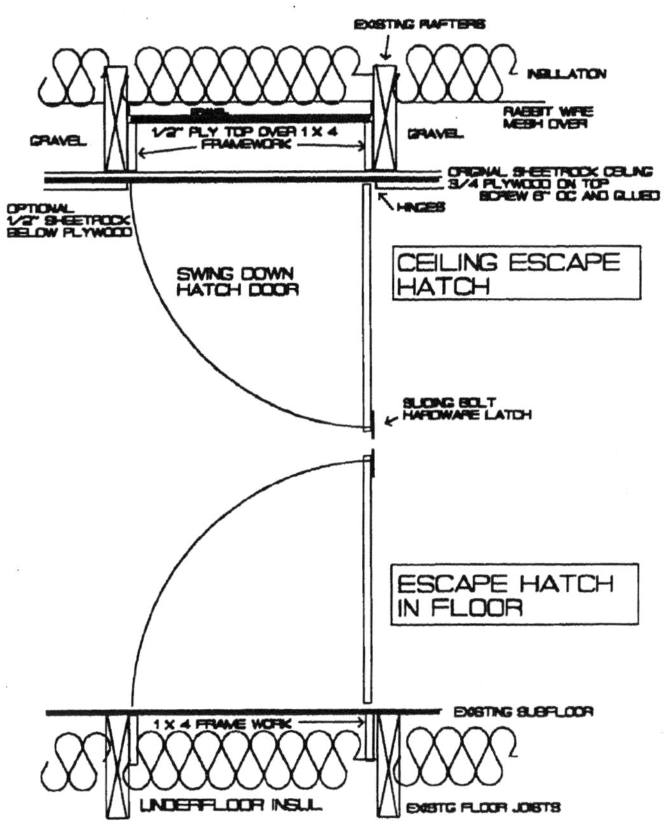

FIGURE 6:

EMERGENCY EXITS

CONCEALED CABINET

If you opt to do a closet within a closet as depicted here, you will want to build a cabinet to conceal the entrance to this inner higher security closet. I have detailed in figure 4 one way of doing this. It is a standard shoe type closet, about 10 inches deep and at least as tall and wide as the door opening you want to cover. Don't make it much wider--just enough to completely cover the door opening. Install a full length heavy duty piano hinge along the long side, so that the pivot edge of the hinge is just flush with the outside edge of the cabinet. If it is too far past the edge the hinge will show, if too far in, the cabinet will not open all the way. Set the cabinet bottom as close to the carpet without touching, so that no sweep marks will be left on the carpet indicating that the cabinet is openable.

If using a metal door jamb, use a portable arc welder to weld a regular 1/4 inch by 3" bolt to the jamb with the head protruding past the finished wall about 9/16 th of an inch. If you want to make the bolt adjustable, attach two nuts to the bolt, so that one is screwed on to the bolt near the front of the door jamb and the other nut is near the end of the bolt. Now weld the nuts to the jamb. Once you adjust the bolt in or out to the correct depth, you can put silicone caulk on the threads to keep it from turning. If you use a wood jamb, weld the nuts to a metal plate and then screw the plate to the jamb. Now blacken the end of the bolt and swing the cabinet back up against it to mark where it makes contact. Now drill a hole in the back of the cabinet large enough so that the bolt comes through the hole without rubbing when the cabinet is closed. Set a shelf support just below this hole such that when a 3/4 inch shelf lays on the supports, it will just cover this bolt. You will have to notch out the bottom of the shelf so that it fits freely over the bolt. Now, recess and attach a short metal plate on the back edge of the shelf with a slot cut part way into it--just wide enough and deep enough to allow it to fit over the back of the bolt head, as seen in figure 4. Thus when the shelf is in place, this metal plate will keep the bolt from being withdrawn out the back of the cabinet if someone tries to open it. Cut another slot in the back, at the same height as the shelf so that if you want to shut yourself into the inner chamber you can do so by using a nail to raise the shelf from behind and drop it in place over the bolt--you will also need to use it to remove the shelf again to get out (very important).

DOOR CROSS BARS: Cross bars should be used on at least the main closet door in order to keep you safe inside during a forced intrusion. If you don't have a bullet proof steel plate on the door, keep away to either side of the door so the gravel in the walls can protect you against any shots an intruder may fire. He or she may become very frustrated and angry at not being able to get in, and may try to shoot out the locks. This is another reason for having the door cross bars. If you use metal jambs, weld the cross bar brackets to the jambs. If you have wood jambs, use two lag bolts on each bracket, and make sure they go into solid wood at least 2 inches.

THE MULTI-PURPOSE HIGH SECURITY VAULT

WORKING DRAWINGS

PLANS

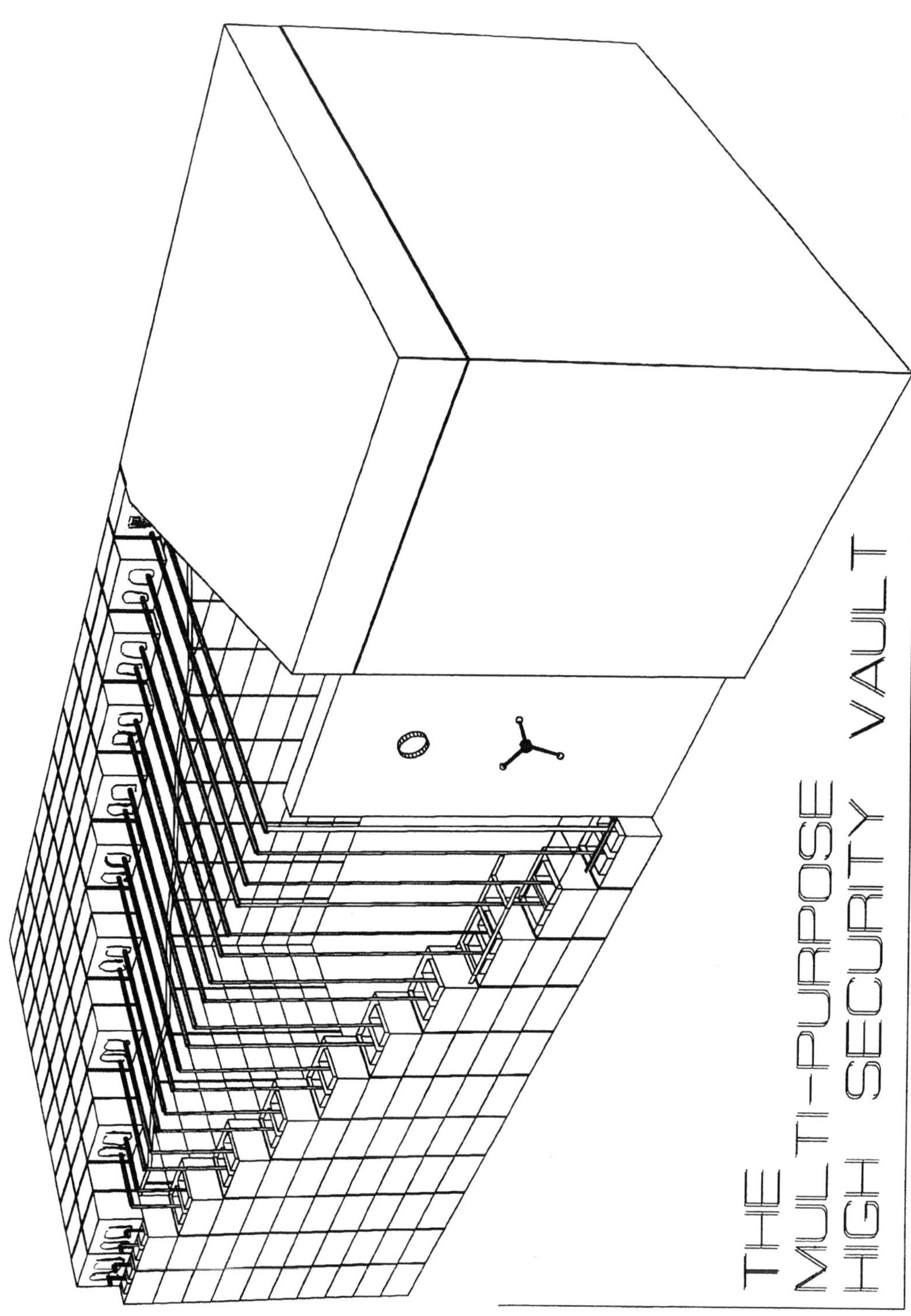

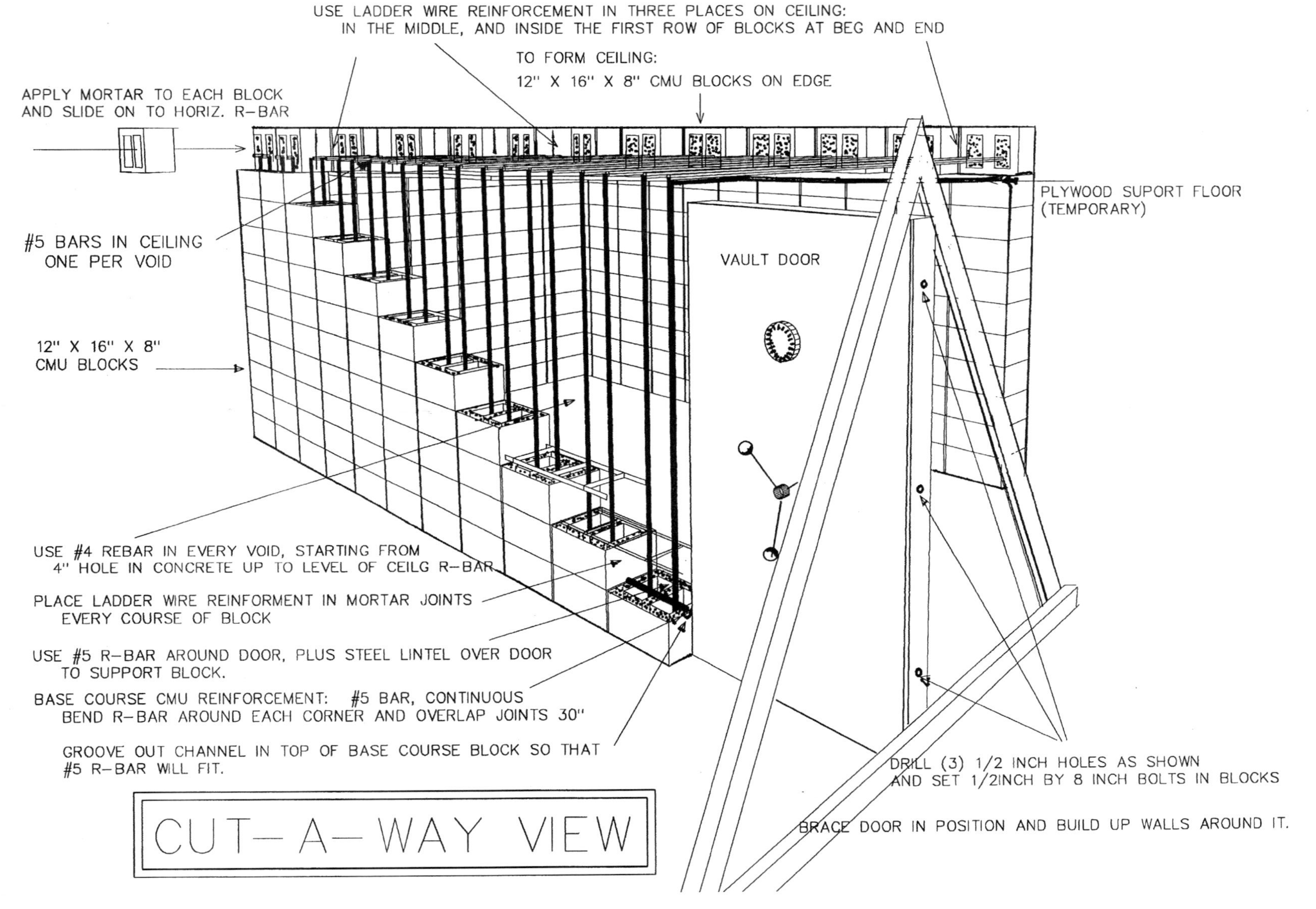
USE LADDER WIRE REINFORCEMENT IN THREE PLACES ON CEILING:
IN THE MIDDLE, AND INSIDE THE FIRST ROW OF BLOCKS AT BEG AND END
TO FORM CEILING:
12" X 16" X 8" CMU BLOCKS ON EDGE
APPLY MORTAR TO EACH BLOCK
AND SLIDE ON TO HORIZ. R-BAR
PLYWOOD SUPORT FLOOR
(TEMPORARY)
#5 BARS IN CEILING
ONE PER VOID
VAULT DOOR
12" X 16" X 8"
CMU BLOCKS
USE #4 REBAR IN EVERY VOID, STARTING FROM
4" HOLE IN CONCRETE UP TO LEVEL OF CEILG R-BAR
PLACE LADDER WIRE REINFORMENT IN MORTAR JOINTS
EVERY COURSE OF BLOCK
USE #5 R-BAR AROUND DOOR, PLUS STEEL LINTEL OVER DOOR
TO SUPPORT BLOCK.
BASE COURSE CMU REINFORCEMENT: #5 BAR, CONTINUOUS
BEND R-BAR AROUND EACH CORNER AND OVERLAP JOINTS 30"
GROOVE OUT CHANNEL IN TOP OF BASE COURSE BLOCK SO THAT
#5 R-BAR WILL FIT.
DRILL (3) 1/2 INCH HOLES AS SHOWN
AND SET 1/2INCH BY 8 INCH BOLTS IN BLOCKS
BRACE DOOR IN POSITION AND BUILD UP WALLS AROUND IT.
CUT-A-WAY VIEW

HIGH SECURITY SHELTER

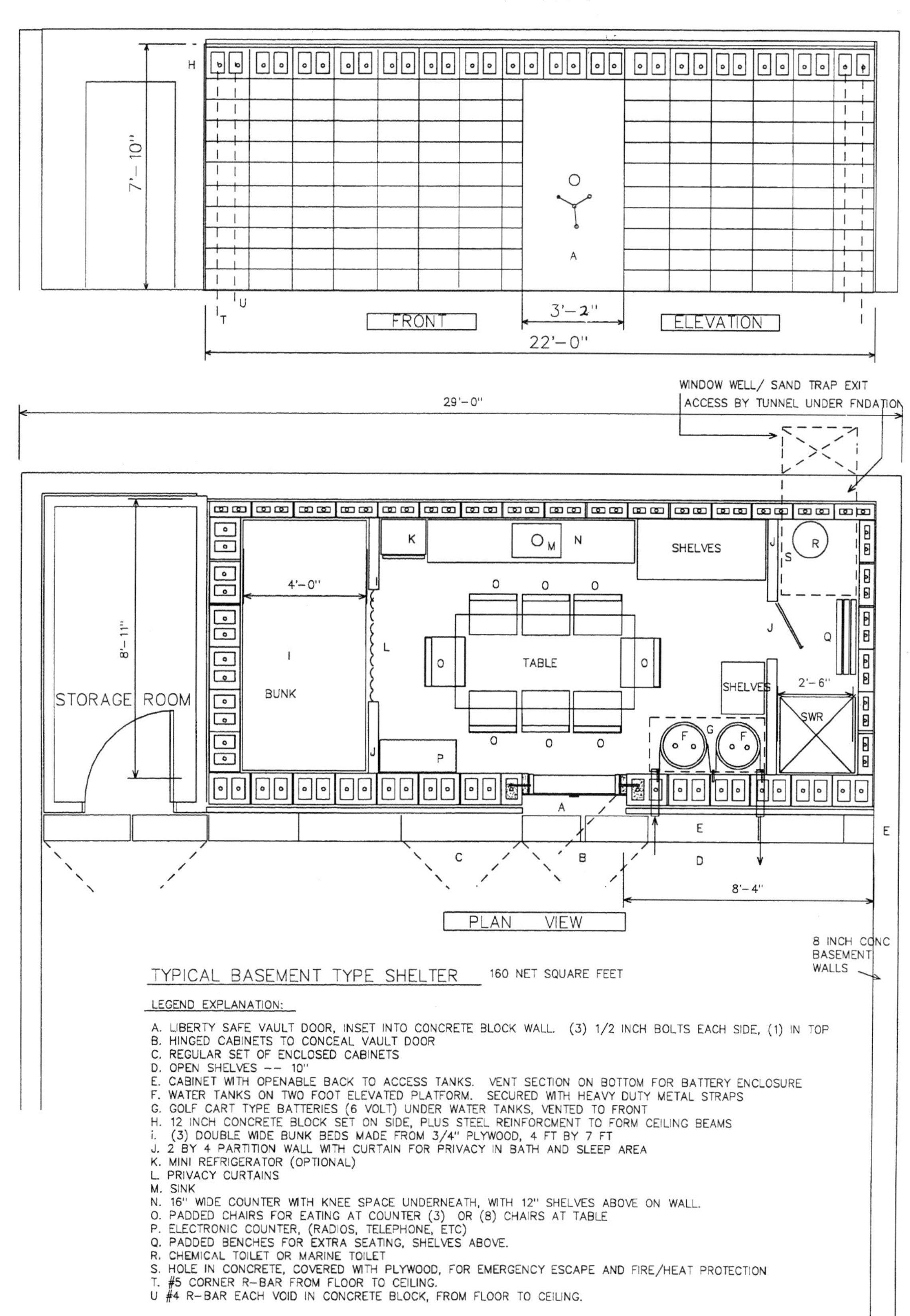

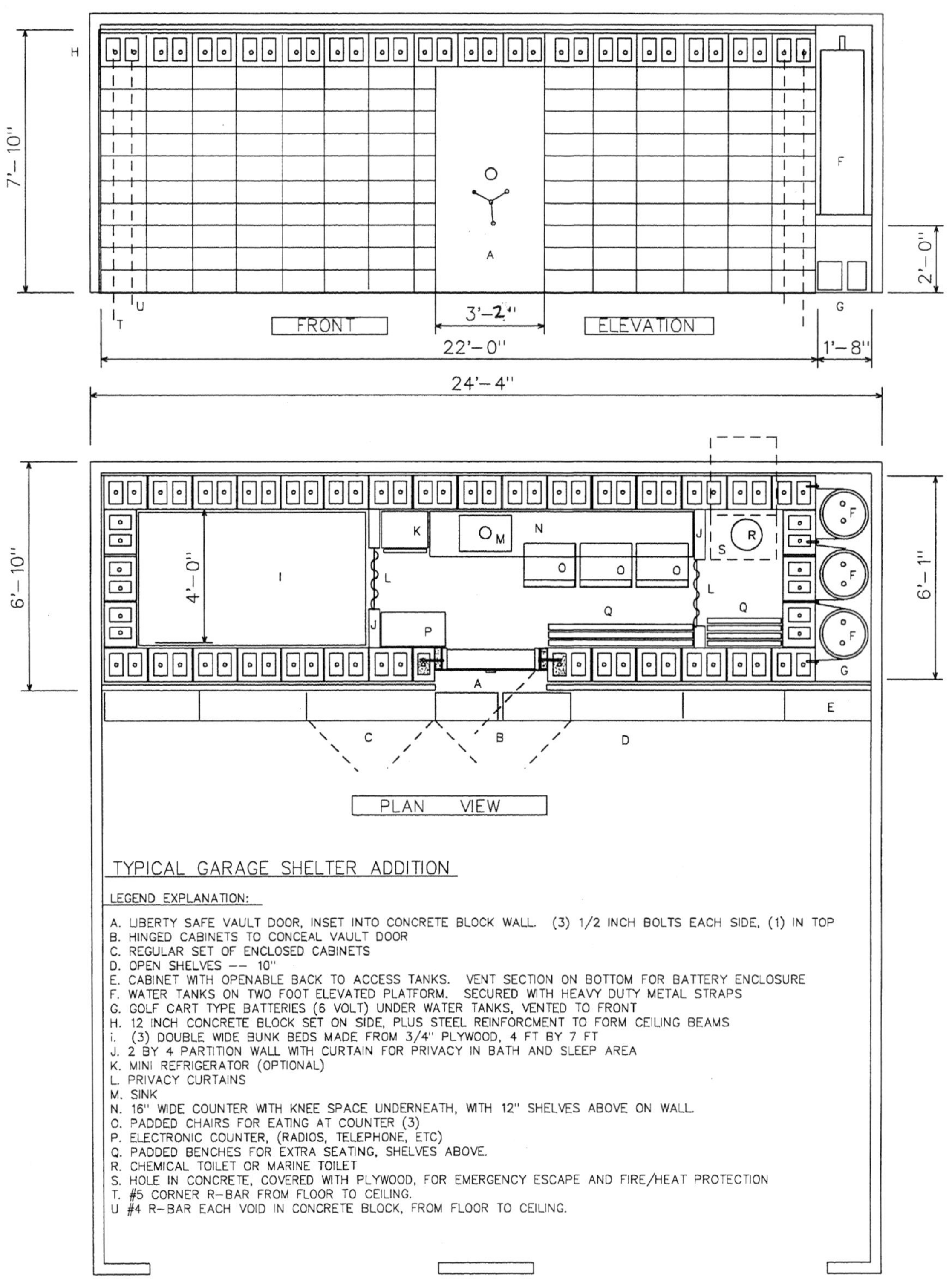
H
F
A
G
7'– 10"
2'– 0"
T
U
FRONT
3'–2"
ELEVATION
22'–0"
1'–8"
24'–4"
6'– 10"
4'–0"
I
K
M
N
O
L
J
P
Q
R
S
6'– 1"
E
C
B
D
PLAN VIEW
TYPICAL GARAGE SHELTER ADDITION
LEGEND EXPLANATION:
A. LIBERTY SAFE VAULT DOOR, INSET INTO CONCRETE BLOCK WALL. (3) 1/2 INCH BOLTS EACH SIDE, (1) IN TOP
B. HINGED CABINETS TO CONCEAL VAULT DOOR
C. REGULAR SET OF ENCLOSED CABINETS
D. OPEN SHELVES -- 10"
E. CABINET WITH OPENABLE BACK TO ACCESS TANKS. VENT SECTION ON BOTTOM FOR BATTERY ENCLOSURE
F. WATER TANKS ON TWO FOOT ELEVATED PLATFORM. SECURED WITH HEAVY DUTY METAL STRAPS
G. GOLF CART TYPE BATTERIES (6 VOLT) UNDER WATER TANKS, VENTED TO FRONT
H. 12 INCH CONCRETE BLOCK SET ON SIDE, PLUS STEEL REINFORCMENT TO FORM CEILING BEAMS
i. (3) DOUBLE WIDE BUNK BEDS MADE FROM 3/4" PLYWOOD, 4 FT BY 7 FT
J. 2 BY 4 PARTITION WALL WITH CURTAIN FOR PRIVACY IN BATH AND SLEEP AREA
K. MINI REFRIGERATOR (OPTIONAL)
L. PRIVACY CURTAINS
M. SINK
N. 16" WIDE COUNTER WITH KNEE SPACE UNDERNEATH, WITH 12" SHELVES ABOVE ON WALL.
O. PADDED CHAIRS FOR EATING AT COUNTER (3)
P. ELECTRONIC COUNTER, (RADIOS, TELEPHONE, ETC)
Q. PADDED BENCHES FOR EXTRA SEATING, SHELVES ABOVE.
R. CHEMICAL TOILET OR MARINE TOILET
S. HOLE IN CONCRETE, COVERED WITH PLYWOOD, FOR EMERGENCY ESCAPE AND FIRE/HEAT PROTECTION
T. #5 CORNER R-BAR FROM FLOOR TO CEILING.
U #4 R-BAR EACH VOID IN CONCRETE BLOCK, FROM FLOOR TO CEILING.

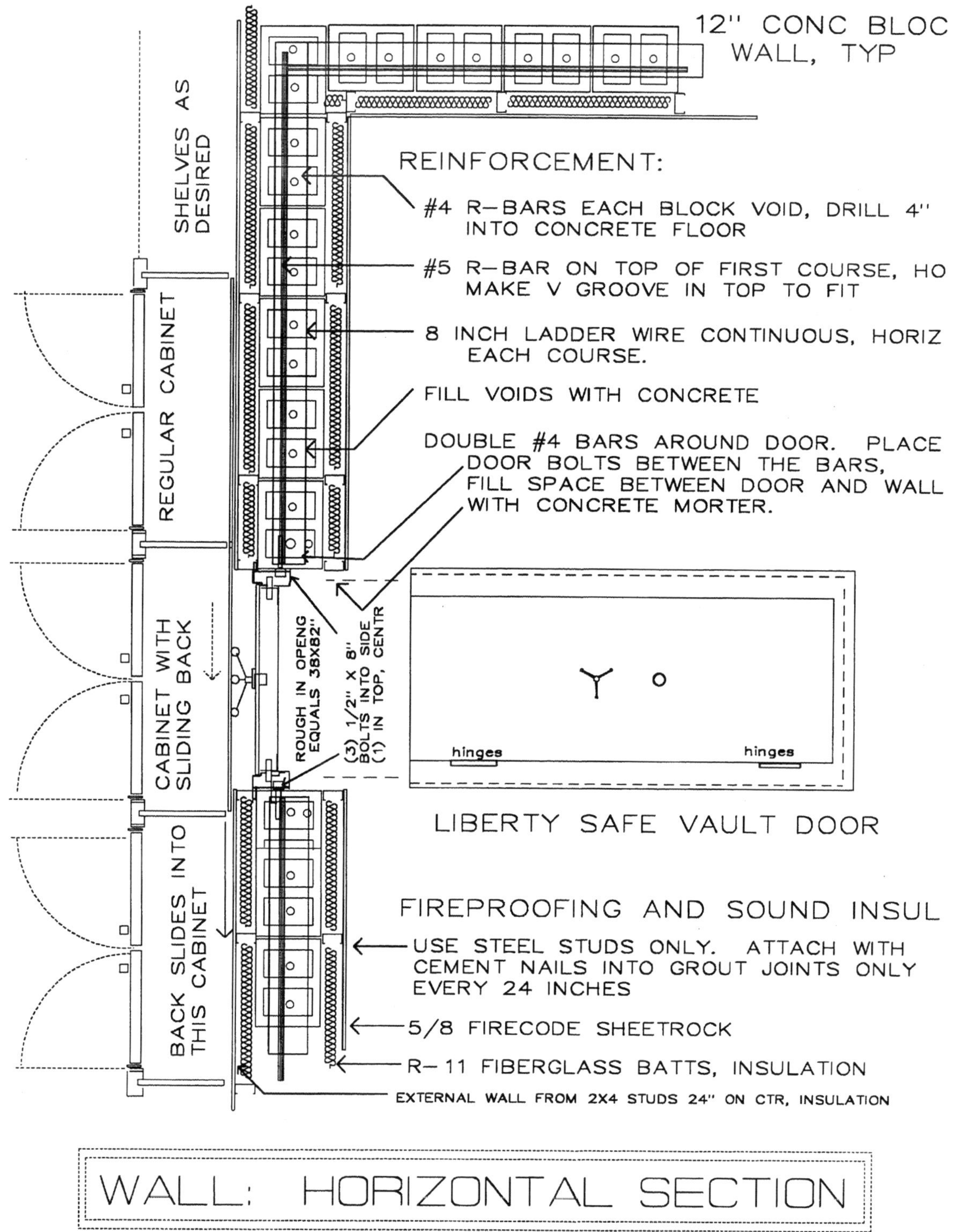

WALL: HORIZONTAL SECTION

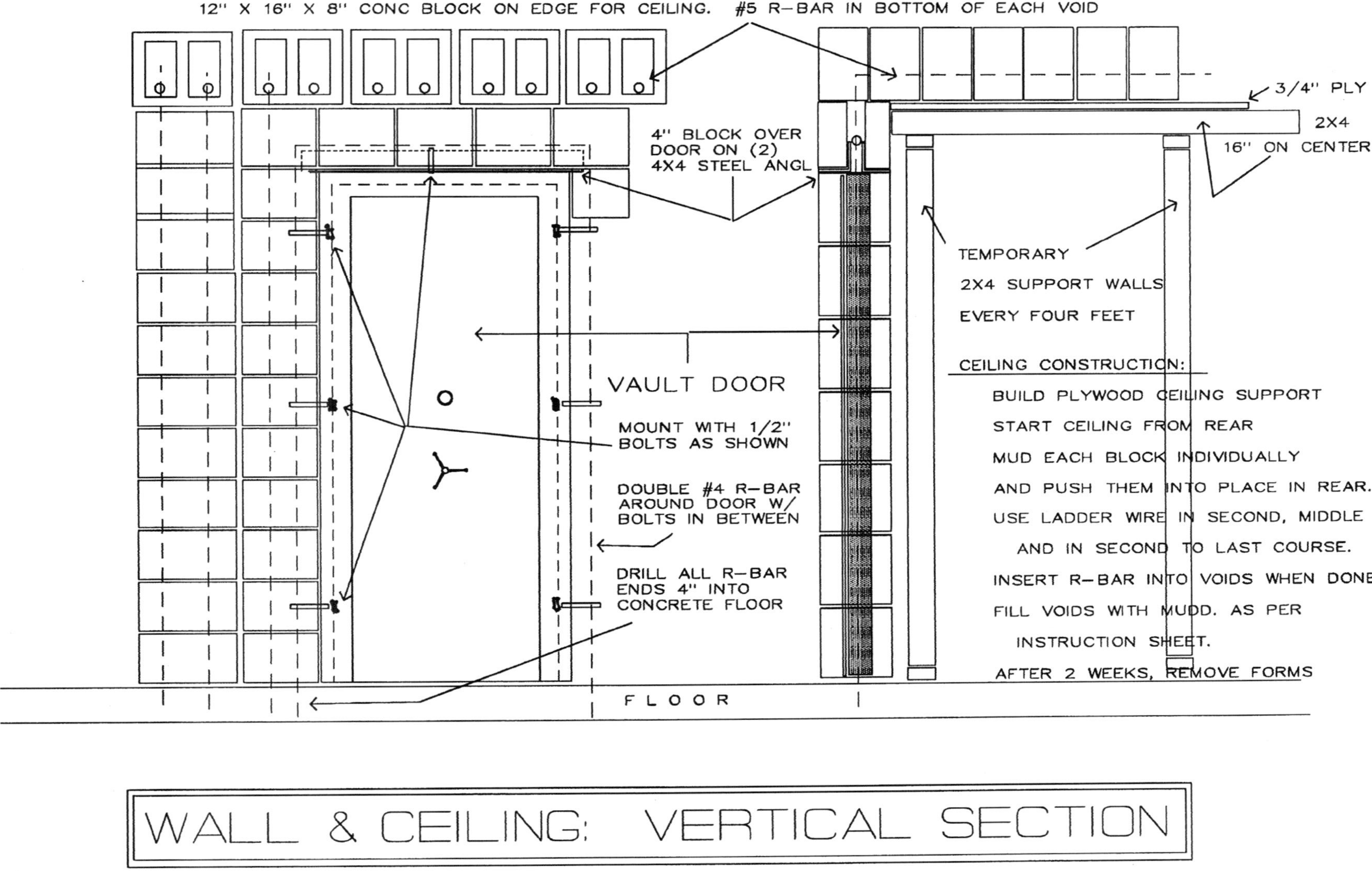
12" X 16" X 8" CONC BLOCK ON EDGE FOR CEILING. #5 R-BAR IN BOTTOM OF EACH VOID
4" BLOCK OVER DOOR ON (2) 4X4 STEEL ANGL
3/4" PLY
2X4
16" ON CENTER
TEMPORARY
2X4 SUPPORT WALLS
EVERY FOUR FEET
VAULT DOOR
MOUNT WITH 1/2" BOLTS AS SHOWN
DOUBLE #4 R-BAR AROUND DOOR W/ BOLTS IN BETWEEN
DRILL ALL R-BAR ENDS 4" INTO CONCRETE FLOOR
CEILING CONSTRUCTION:
BUILD PLYWOOD CEILING SUPPORT
START CEILING FROM REAR
MUD EACH BLOCK INDIVIDUALLY
AND PUSH THEM INTO PLACE IN REAR.
USE LADDER WIRE IN SECOND, MIDDLE
AND IN SECOND TO LAST COURSE.
INSERT R-BAR INTO VOIDS WHEN DONE.
FILL VOIDS WITH MUDD. AS PER
INSTRUCTION SHEET.
AFTER 2 WEEKS, REMOVE FORMS
FLOOR
WALL & CEILING: VERTICAL SECTION

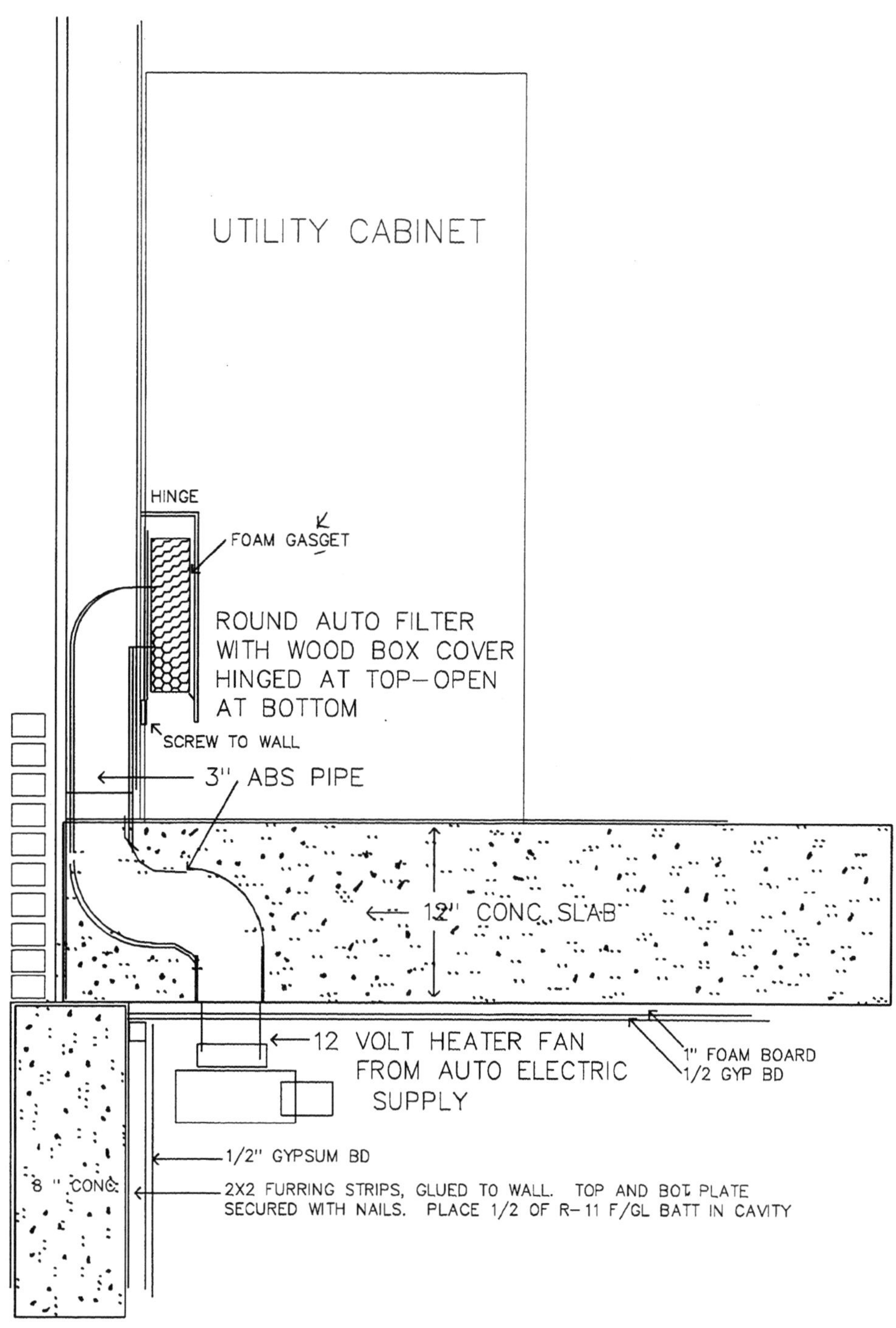

AIR VENT/FILTRATION (INLET SIDE)
FOR SHELTER UNDER AN EXISTING ROOM (GARAGE)

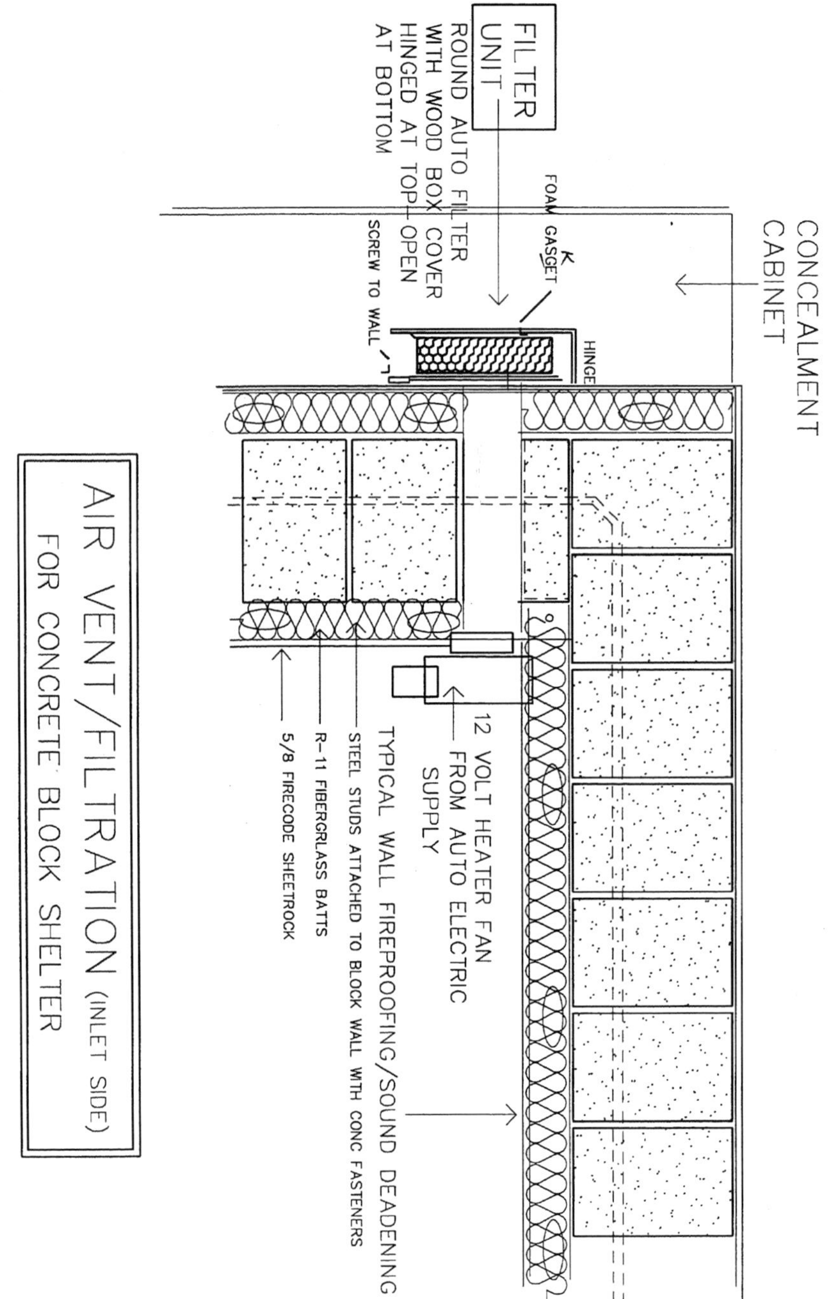
FILTER UNIT
ROUND AUTO FILTER WITH WOOD BOX COVER HINGED AT TOP—OPEN AT BOTTOM
FOAM GASKET
HINGE
SCREW TO WALL
CONCEALMENT CABINET
12 VOLT HEATER FAN FROM AUTO ELECTRIC SUPPLY
TYPICAL WALL FIREPROOFING/SOUND DEADENING
STEEL STUDS ATTACHED TO BLOCK WALL WITH CONC FASTENERS
R-11 FIBERGRLASS BATTS
5/8 FIRECODE SHEETROCK
AIR VENT/FILTRATION (INLET SIDE)
FOR CONCRETE BLOCK SHELTER

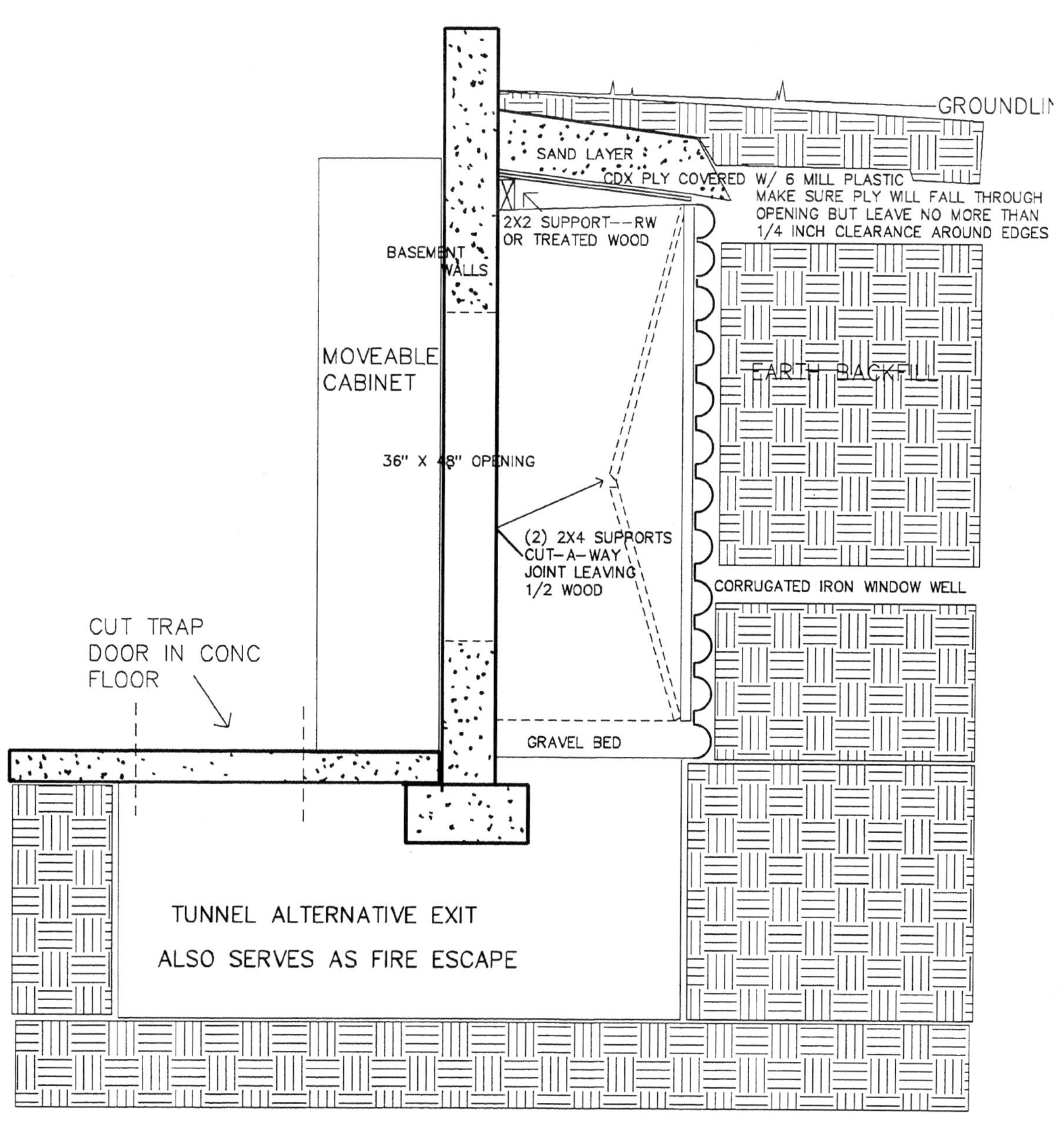

SAND TRAP EXIT

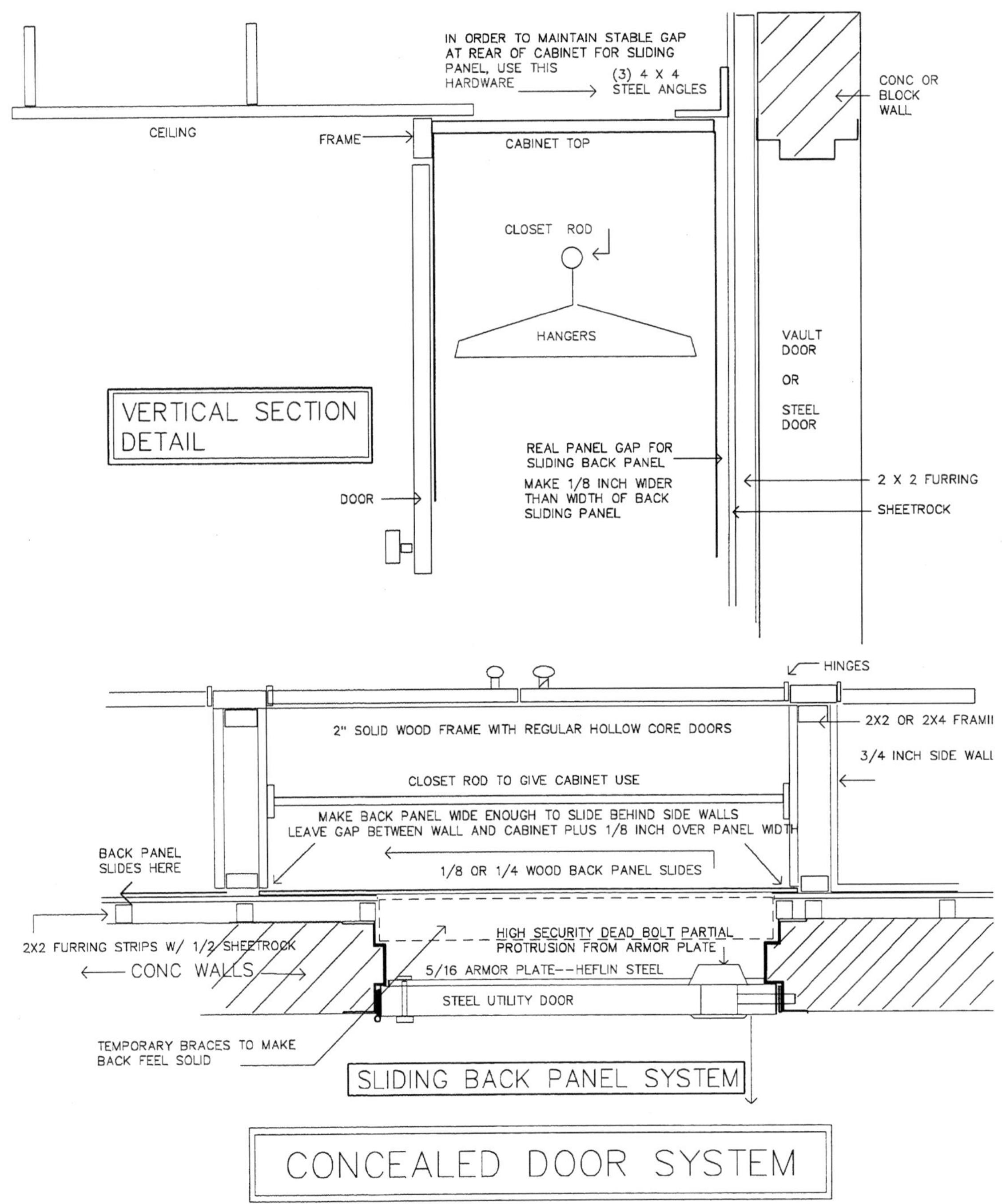

CONCEALED DOOR SYSTEM

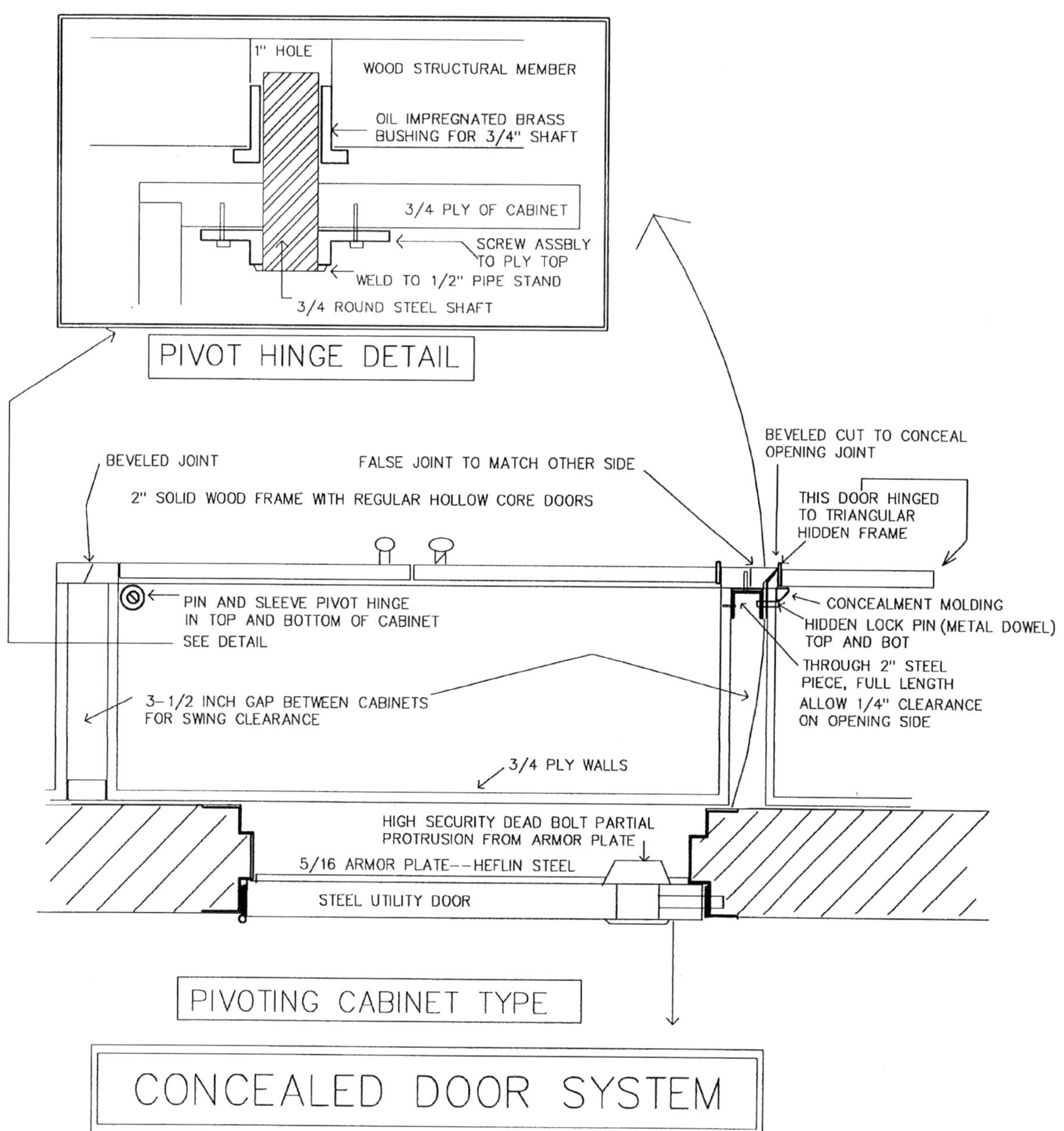

CONCEALED DOOR SYSTEM

PRODUCT SUPPLIERS

Here is a list of suppliers who carry a variety of items mentioned in this list. To save space, I will only mention their name as a source within the list, instead of giving out their address and telephone numbers each time they are mentioned. Check here for contact information if it isn't listed in the body of the list. In most cases I will try and give an Internet website URL (URL means an Internet address, usually preceded by a www). Going to a company website will allow you to view the product and read important information. This will save you much time and effort.

ABRAHAM SOLAR EQUIPMENT: This is my top recommended source for all your solar and alternate energy products. Mick has low prices and he knows all the equipment personally, including how to install it. Above everything, I can personally vouch for Mick Abraham's honesty and integrity. This is a source you can completely trust. Order line: 1-800-222-7242, Consultation (970) 731-4675; address: 124 Creekside Place, Pagosa Springs, Co. 81147. Website: www.abrahamsolar.com

BE SELF RELIANT.COM: This is company with a lot of practical experience in designing and installing self-sufficient and multi-fuel systems within homes. They are based out of Idaho and are quickly developing into a comprehensive one-stop resource for self-sufficiency products and information. This includes: alternative energy, heating, home production, self-reliant skills development, consulting, and installation. They have developed a unique home heating boiler system that uses any available fuel, simply by changing out the burner. It also uses coal and wood. I don't know of any other system that matches this one. All of their systems come with extensive "How To" documentation for the do-it-yourselfer. Phone: (208) 624-3135 or (888) 624-0040 website: www.beselfreliant.com Email: info@beselfreliant.com

EMERGENCY ESSENTIALS: Largest of the Utah-based full service preparedness products stores. Website www.beprepared.com : 653 North 1500 West, Orem, Utah 84057 Phone contact numbers: 1-801-222-9596-Corporate offices, 1-801-222-9598 Fax
1-800-999-1863 Customer order line. Email: sales@beprepared.com

PROVIDENT LIVING: Excellent online shopping for 72 hour kits and specialty preparedness equipment. They also sell a full range of storage foods. Website: http://www.providentlivingcenter.com/

MAJOR SURPLUS AND SURVIVAL: Biggest of the California survival food and products stores. Website URL: http://www.majorsurplusnsurvival.com / . Address: 435 W. Alondra Blvd.; Gardena, Ca 90248 Tel: (800)441-8855 or (310)324-8855 email: sales@MajorSurplusNSurvival.com

NITRO-PAK: Carries a full line of survival foods and products. Website: http://www.nitro-pak.com /

WALTON FEED: Largest of the survival food suppliers. Website: http://waltonfeed.com/ Location: 135 North 10th (PO Box 307) Montpelier ID 83254 Phone: 800-847-0465
LEHMAN'S CATALOG: The largest of the self-sufficient/back-to-the-land suppliers. Website: www.lehmans.com . Address: Lehman's Non-Electric Catalog Listing ID 575. Phone: 1-877 438-5346 Email: info@lehmans.com Mail: Lehman's, 289 Kurzen Road North Dalton, Ohio 44618

REAL GOODS: California and Colorado outlets for full range of back-to-the-land and self-sufficiency products. Website: http://www.gaiam.com/realgoods/default.htm/

HIGH SECURITY SHELTER

AMATEUR ELECTRONIC SUPPLY (AES): Biggest of the mail order Ham radio and antenna stores. Website: http://www.aesham.com / Order their catalog: 1-800-558-0411.

HAM RADIO OUTLET: 1-800-644-4476 (east) or 1-800-854-6046 (west). Major competitor or AES. Website: www.hamradio.com/ Order their catalog 1-800-444-0047

RADIO SHACK: website www.radioshack.com . Nationwide electronics parts, radios, telephones, and security systems. Order line: 1-800-843-7422 (get a catalog at local store or see it online).

WW GRAINGER: Nationwide wholesalers of almost every type of equipment. You must have some type of business in order to establish a wholesale account with them, but it is worth it. Check their website for the warehouse nearest you: www.grainger.com .

NORTHERN TOOL AND EQUIPMENT: Major discount mail-order catalog company for generators and major tools and equipment. Website: http://www.northerntool.com / or 1-800-221-0516

HOME IMPROVEMENT STORES TO PURCHASE ITEMS AT A DISCOUNT

COSTCO WHOLESALE: See website for location of stores nearest you: www.costco.com . They are in most states East and West (but only a few in the Midwest (Illinois, Indiana, Iowa, and Kansas). Chain discount bulk supplies of household products and services. Very high quality and cheap prices.

SAM'S CLUB (WALMART CHAIN): Nationwide chain carrying bulk supplies at discount prices.

HOME DEPOT: Largest national home improvement store chain. Website URL: www.homedepot.com .

LOWES: Nationwide home improvement discount store; second largest in the nation. They are better than Home Depot for specialty tools and hardware. Website: www.lowes.com

LISTINGS

CONSTRUCTION MATERIALS AND EQUIPMENT
GROUND SOURCE HEAT PUMPS
International Ground Source Heat Pump Association: http://www.igshpa.okstate.edu / Has a listing of many approved installers.
WaterFurnace International, Inc. 9000 Conservation Way, Fort Wayne, IN 46809 USA
Website: http://www.waterfurnace.com Tel: 800-436-7283.

PLASTIC LUMBER DECKING Now available at all home building stores.

STEEL DECKING FOR FORMING UP SHELTER CEILINGS: Many brands of steel decking are available at local steel suppliers in most large cities. Deal locally to avoid shipping costs.
FormDeck Comes 36" wide in variety of lengths. Contact Structures of USA, P.O. Box 639 Johnstown, PA 15907 Tel: 814-536-8371 URL: http://www.structuresofusa.com /

HIGH SECURITY SHELTER

SHATTERPROOF WINDOWS AND SKYLIGHTS

Roto Frank (German made) high strength skylights. Website: www.rotohardware.com/ Available in US at skylight distributors.

Andersen Windows makes a triple laminate glass with polymer layers in between. These windows are intrusion-proof, and will not scratch like Shattergard film. This is the glass system they use on their high strength (hurricane-proof) skylites. You can order this glass in their regular window line as well. Cost is about 30% higher than standard glass/wood windows. Andersen Windows (available at window suppliers everywhere).

STAIR-STEPPED MODULAR WINDOW WELL (for fire escape)

Scapewell by The Bilco Company: URL: www.bilco.com. The Bilco Company, P.O. Box 1203, New Haven, Connecticut 06505 Tel: 203-934-6363.

INSULATING WINDOW FILMS/INSULATION

Gila Films have a full range of energy saving films to apply to windows. Website: http://www.gilafilms.com /

QUILTED DECORATIVE INSULATING CURTAINS FOR SOLAR WINDOWS

See the Website of 1WindowQuilts.com: http://www.1windowquilts.com/ They sell a rolling shutter type installation that is easy to install.

FOIL INSULATION

One of the latest innovations is bubble Poly blankets with foil on front and back. It's great for molding into window jambs or stapling to attic rafters, or cover existing attic insulation to reflect summer heat and keep winter heat inside. Website: http://www.reflectixinc.com/ But it is sold in stores everywhere no--even on Amazon.com.

SOUND INSULATION

Insul-Tek and O.E.M. Sound Deadener, self adhesive automotive stype sound-proofing. This is very compact, effective material. Call Juliano's to order. Orders: 800-300-1932 Technical Assistance: 860-872-1932. Insul-Tek 1/4" thick core of polyethylene foam with aluminum foil bonded to both sides. Will not absorb moisture. Reduces noise level by 40%. Website: http://www.julianos.com/insultek.html/

SONEX Professional quality deep finger foam for shooting ranges. Ilbruck Inc, 3800 Washington Ave North Minneapolis, Mn 55412. Tel (612) 521-3555. website: http://www.illbruck-sonex.com /

ADD-ON PROTECTIVE FILMS

Shattergard Protective Film (unbreakable backing to standard glass). Itcan be applied to existing house and car windows. Makes windows bullet-proof to small caliber (.22) weapons and makes windows impenetrable to intruders. www.shattergard.com .

FIREPROOF SHEETROCK

In the 1980's a woman invented real fireproof plaster that was vastly superior to type XX sheetrock (which merely sloughs off during a fire. The product is called GEOBOND, and comes in panels as well as a stucco-like exterior coating. It can be used in combination with many other materials. Website: www.geobond.net (inactive site) This is a truly amazing family of products, but it looks like it was not a commercial success and may not be available now.

HIGH SECURITY SHELTER

FIREPROOF PLYWOOD

Plycem. This is a recycled material which has higher densities than all other sheathings. It is marketed by Castleblock P.O. Box 1893, Ventura, CA USA 93002 Tel: 800-672-7872 Website: http://www.castleblock.com/

STRUCTURAL BUILDING PANELS

R-Control Structural Building Panels. factory-made wall systems that replace wall framing. Also R-Control Speclam (insulation foam attached to particle board) AFM Corp24000 West Highway 7, P.O. Box 246 Excelsior, MN 55331 Tel: 1-800-255-0176. (612) 474-0809 or 1-800-255-0176 Fax: 612-474-2074. Website: http://www.afmcorp-epsfoam.com/

EIFS (EXTERIOR INSULATED FINISH SYSTEMS)

Exterior insulated finish systems (EIFS) consist of synthetic stucco applied over insulation board, which is then installed over sheathing. These systems have been used commercially for years, but they received some bad press recently when homeowners complained that these systems were failing. Moisture penetrated the wall and the sheathing and structural members rotted. While manufacturers, contractors, and homeowners swap complaints, drainable siding is entering the picture. Manufacturers say that this system allows moisture that gets behind the stucco to drain harmlessly to the outside.
Dryvit: website: dryvit.com. Tel: 800-556-7752. Dryvit Systems, Inc. One Energy Way, P.O. Box 1014 West Warwick, RI 02893.
Pleko See website at www.pleko.com/ (Dryvit substitute; more competitive in price.)

CHEAPER ALTERNATIVE TO EIFS

The QUIKRETE® Hardcoat Stucco System provides builders and contractors with unparalleled durability and moisture protection that is lacking in Exterior Insulation and Finish Systems (EIFS). The Hardcoat Stucco System is comprised of QUIKRETE Liquid Stucco decorative coating over a base coat of QUIKRETE Fiberglass-Reinforced Stucco. Unlike EIFS, where water may become trapped between a synthetic finish coat and the interior drywall, Fiberglass-Reinforced Stucco acts as a drainage medium. If water penetrates the top coat of Liquid Stucco, it will migrate down the base coat and out through a flashing at the concrete footing. The Hardcoat Stucco System combines the design versatility and energy efficiency of EIFS with the durability and water drainage benefits of cement-based systems. Fiberglass-Reinforced Stucco is reinforced with alkali-resistant glass fibers. It provides a high impact, crack-resistant shell and can be trowel or spray-applied at a 3/8-inch thickness using wire mesh over insulation board or sheathing. Fiberglass-Reinforced Stucco also provides the ideal base for the Liquid Stucco decorative coating, which is a moisture-resistant color and texture coating designed for use over concrete and stucco surfaces. This ready-to-use and trowel-applied product is a 100 percent acrylic co-polymer-based coating. It is available in swirl, coarse sand, and fine sand textures and can be pigmented to any desired color, thus offering unlimited design options. This system can also be used over the concrete stack-block method. URL: www.quickcrete.com .

ELECTRICAL, MISC

GFCI (Ground Fault Circuit Interrupter). Installing a GFCI outlet for your washing machine for shock protection is worthwhile. However, some GFCIs might trip every time the motor is activated. To prevent this type of nuisance tripping, the Leviton Manufacturing Co. indicated that you should get the Hospital

Grade GFCI outlet rather than the regular commercial grade. The catalog number of this part is 6598-HG, and it's available at commercial electrical supply stores.

GREENHOUSE MANUFACTURERS AND COMPONENTS
Conley's Mfg. & Sales 4344 E. Mission Blvd., Montclair, CA 91763 Tel: 909-627-0981 URL: www.conley.com (a commercial greenhouse manufacturer. Will send components to you as well as twinwall glazing at wholesale rates).
Nexus Corp. 10983 Leroy Drive Northglenn, CO 80233 Tel: 303-457-9199 URL: www.nexus.com/ (A commercial greenhouse manufacturer. Will sell components to you as well as twinwall glazing at wholesale rates).

PLASTIC GREENHOUSE FILM
Armin Plastics Corp. 18901 East Railroad Street City of Industry, CA 91748 Tel: 800-654-8119 URL: www.armin.com/ (supplies a full range of single layer plastic, UV protected greenhouse coverings - suitable for warmer climates.

STRUCTURAL METAL COMPONENTS (aluminum square tubing, round tubing etc)
Allied Tube & Conduit 16100 S. Lathrop Ave. Harvey, IL 60426 Tel: 800-882-5543 URL: www.allied.com/ . Also available at steel/metal supply houses in all major cities.

DEHUMIDIFYING AIR TO AIR HEAT EXCHANGERS
HEAT WHEELS by XeteX, Inc. 3530 E. 28th St.. Minneapolis, MN 55406 Tel: (888) 899-9991 Toll Free. (These unique spinning wheels have water absorbing media on the blades which transfers humidity from incoming fresh air to the outgoing stream of exhaust air.)

WATERPROOFING MATERIALS FOR BASEMENTS, UNDERGROUND HOMES
FIXING BASEMENT CRACKS
Most use hydraulic cement (rigid). For a better job, fill the crack on the inside using a tough, but flexible professional-grade sealant such as SIKAFLEX 1A. Prepare the crack according to the manufacturer's instructions, then coat it with Sikaflex primer 429 and apply the Sikaflex-1a. Finish up by covering the repair with SikaTop Seal 107, a polymer-modified, cement-based coating. A 10.3-ounce cartridge of Sikaflex-1a costs about $5, a pint of primer about $12.50 and the SikaTop Seal about $40. Bear in mind that these products are not sold at home centers or hardware stores. They are sold through construction supply houses, some of which are reluctant to sell less than case-size quantities to a homeowner. So the prices of individual cartridges or cans may vary from what we show here. For more information, contact SIKA CORP. 201 Polito Ave., Lyndhurst, NJ 07071; 800-933-7452.

WATERPROOFING WALLS, UNDERGROUND ROOFS:
Black Hills Bentonite Box 9, Mills, Wyoming 82644 URL www.bhbentonite.com Email: bhbentonite@doccee.com. You can also find bentonite pellets at almost any well drilling outfit.

Paraseal (HDPE) Waterproofing Membrane (from W.R. Grace Co, and national firm. Local construction firms can get this product). Paraseal is a dual combination of two of the most effective waterproofing materials, high density polyethylene (HDPE) and bentonite clay, laminated together to form a tough, single sheet membrane. It is easily installed and typically applied on backfilled wall conditions, under floors, decks, or as a pond liner. The Paraseal dual membrane system is also available in a lagging grade,

HIGH SECURITY SHELTER

Paraseal LG, which is designed for blindside installations or where shotcrete is to be blown directly into the face of the membrane.
Bituthene Heavy duty waterproof membranes that can literally surround the outside of a basement (even under slabs and footings) to make a basement waterproof in a high water table area. Bituthene 1000x by W.R. Grace Co. (available through local concrete contractors).

Vulkem 201/222 are also ideal for waterproofing foundation walls. By Tremco Incorporated 3735 Green Rd., Beachwood, OH 44122 Tel: 216-292-5000 or 800-321-7906.
Underground roofs: Apply 30 or 45 mil EPDM rubber pond liner material over Polyurethane foam sprayed on insulation. Pond liners widely available at rural farm stores.

WATERPROOFING FOR DECKS
Vulkem #350/351 Pedestrian Deck Coating System. Tremco Incorporated 3735 Green Rd. Beachwood, OH 44122 Tel: 216-292-5000 or 800-321-7906.

CUPOLAS (special decorative vent housings that go on top of traditional styled roofs and barns)
Stephenson Cupolas and Weathervanes. Nashville Sash and Door, Tel: (615) 254-1371
Edon Fiberglass Cupolas. 1-800-255-0176, URL www.edon.com/ (These are indestructible vents and never need maintenance).

CONSTRUCTION TYPES: ALTERNATIVE

INFORMATION ON CONCRETE HOMES
www.concretehomes.com/

PRECAST CONCRETE
Thermomass Residential Building Systems. (The best residential system in the world - uses a thermal sandwich of foam in between two concrete precast surfaces. Has heat mass characteristics, rodents cannot get into the foam layer, bullet-proof, and the best sound-proofing available) 1999 Highview Rd. Coralville, IA 52241 Tel: (319) 351-4232 Fax (319) 351-0993 Website: www.t-mass.com .
Kistner Concrete Products, Inc. (Prefab security buildings, precast basement foundation systems) They also have very innovative retaining wall systems with planting areas. 8713 Read Road East Pembroke, NY 14056 Tel: 716-762-8216 Fax: 716-762-8315 Website: www.kistner.com .
Tierra Concrete Homes P.O. Box 1924, Pueblo, CO Tel: 719-947-3040 Fax: 719-947-3050. Website: http://www.tierraconcretehomes.com/service.html/

Oldcastle Precast Custom precast water-proof concrete tanks. Can combine these to make drop-in-the-ground shelter systems. Contact: Oldcastle Products, 2820 A Street, SE Auburn, WA 98071-0608 Tel: 253-833-2777 Fax: 253-939-9126 or 888-232-6274. Website: www.oldcastle-precast.com/ They have local manufacturers all over the USA.

PRECAST CONCRETE SLABS (AIR CORE CONCRETE)
For use as flooring systems or roofing systems. Duct heat or cooling air into the floor tubes. FLEXICORE brand slabs are available in all states. Check with commercial concrete contractors in every major city. Example: http://www.flexicoreoftexas.com/

THERMAL MASS CONCRETE BLOCK CONSTRUCTION

The Natural Home Source: These designers and builders have the most experience in heat mass - passive solar homes. Their system is applicable to most areas of the country, but especially the West. I don't agree with all their techniques or their pricing commissions, but you can learn a lot from their information and implement what you want on your own. They cover waste treatment systems, earth sheltered homes and buildings, solar air heating systems, composting system components, indoor gardening/attached greenhouses. Silverthorne, CO 80498 Tel: 970-262-6727 Website: http://www.thenaturalhome.com/ .

DOME UNDERGROUND HOMES

All of the following companies have been in business over 20 years, so they know what they are doing.

Nest Egg Homes (an underground system using concrete dome or tunnel type structures) Formworks Building, Inc. P.O. Box 1509, Durango, CO 81302 Tel: 970-247-2100 URL: www.formworksbuilding.com.

The Terra-Dome Corp. Underground or bermed buildings. They have tremendous experience in the field. http://www.terra-dome.com/ Hdq: 8908 S. Shrout Rd. Grain Valley, MO 64029 Tel: 1-800.481.3663 toll-free

Davis Caves Construction, Inc. P.O. Box 69, Armington, IL 61721 Website: www.daviscaves.com Tel: 309-392-2574.

CEDAR HOMES

International Homes of Cedar (Laminated Cedar Homes) P.O. Box 886, Woodinville, Wa 98072 Tel: 360-668-8511 or toll free 800-767-7674. Website: http://www.ihoc.com/

LOG HOMES

There are hundreds of log home companies. However, it has been my experience that log home suppliers in the Eastern US are almost double the price of western log home suppliers. Call for price comparison with the company below to see how your local dealer compares. Often it is much cheaper to ship log kits from the west than buy in the east.

Real Log Homes Hartland, VT and throughout the Eastern States (800) 732-5564 Compare prices with the West. Website: http://www.realloghomes.com/

Timberline Log Homes 915 N. State St. Orem, Ut 84058, (801) 226-8786. website: http://www.timberlineloghomes.net/ This is the company I use as a reference for a fair price. I have consistently found this outfit to be very competitive and fairly priced. Check your prices locally and then give the same specs to this company to see how they compare. In many cases, it has been more economical to buy from Timberline, and ship to the East coast than to buy in the East.

ICF (INSULATED CONCRETE FORMS)

The Portland Cement Association has introduced both a book on building with insulated concrete forms (known as ICF construction), and a 5-part video series on the topic. The 326-page book, Insulating Concrete Forms, ($60 postpaid) is a highly detailed look at these systems, from design through installation to completion. Numerous section and perspective views of various ICFs are given. If you're considering building with an ICF system, the book is necessary reading. The video series ($65 postpaid) doesn't provide detailed information, but it gives a realistic overview of ICFs, since much of its 80 minutes was filmed at construction sites. The five videos are design, planning, setting forms, placing concrete, and utilities/interior finish. Contact the Portland Cement Association, 5420 Old Orchard Rd., Skokie, IL 60077.

THERMALITE: 1-800-500-4898. website: http://www.thermaliteforms.com/ . Flat foam forming system tied together with plastic ties. One of few systems that can accommodate concrete walls up to 14 inches wide. One has to put together the forms - do not come as blocks, thus allowing much wider variety of wall widths. Bracing system must be rented or purchased from them - highly recommended.

BLUE MAX: One of the only foam block systems that allows an 8" wide, full-width concrete wall. Now under the name ARXX: website: http://www.arxx.net/
AAB Building System, Inc. http://oikos.com/esb/40/AAB-icf.html Address: 840 Division St., Cobourg, Ontario K9A-4J9 Canada Tel: 800-293-3210 Fax: 905-373-0002.

SMARTBLOCK Use variable width form only - gives solid wall thickness up to 8." Pre formed blocks with integral ties. Plastic ties are built into foam, recessed 3/4" from outside (makes them a little harder to reach for attachment purposes). CONFORM website: http://www.smartblock.com/ Call 1-800-CONFORM for distributor nearest you.

LITEFORM: (Flat foam - have to build it up yourself, so it takes longer) But, you can buy wholesale direct from the factory and save money. Lite-Form International is headquartered at 1210 Steuben St., Sioux City, IA 51105 Tel: 712-252-3704 Fax: 712-252-3259 Toll Free in North America 1-800-551-3313 website: http://www.liteform.com/ . Email: general@liteform.com/

QUADLOCK (Flat Foam forms - install ties yourself) They also have insulated decking for floors and ceilings. Website: www.quadlock.com . Address: QUAD-LOCK Building Systems Ltd. 7398 132nd Street Surrey, B.C. V3W 4M7 Canada Tel: (888) 711-LOCK (604) 590-3111 Fax: (604) 590-8412.

CUSTOM MODULAR HOMES
Avis Homes, Avis, Pa. http://www.avisamerica.com/ Probably the most advance type of modular homes available--with a great deal of customization possible. These are not your normal type of tract home.

STORAGE SHIPPING CONTAINERS (Insulated Reefers) about $2200 plus shipping. Equipment Service Storage 7226 North Loop East Houston, Tx 77028 Tel: 713-674-1082 Dallas Office 214-374-3995. Check locally as well. There are many outlets across the nation for these containers.

DC OR AC ELECTRICAL EQUIPMENT

LOW VOLTAGE LIGHTING SYSTEMS
Lite Touch, Inc One of the premier remote control lighting systems. Great for activating lights and shutters systems remotely--or anything electrical. Tel: 801-268-8668. http://www.litetouch.com/

LINEAR CURRENT BOOSTER (for using solar panels to run a water pump or motor directly)
Sun Selector LCB 20 (about $400) Abraham Solar Equipment

DC LOAD CENTER

HIGH SECURITY SHELTER

Alternate Energy Engineering http://www.aeesolar.com/index.htm/ or talk to Abraham Solar Equip.

AC-DC POWER CONTROL CENTER
Trace Power Center Combines all meters, fuses, circuit breakers, and connections into one unit - code approved. Custom built for each application. Buy from Abraham Solar or Beselfreliant.com

DC-AC SOLID STATE INVERTER

TRACE CORPORATION is NOW XANTREX. They are considered by many to be "top of the Line" but energy guru Mick Abraham says they have now become way too complex. So, now he also sells

VICTRON ENERGY BLUE inverters: Check out the differences. Contact Mick at www.abrahamsolar.com

BATTERY EQUALIZER SYSTEM (for combining 12 volt batteries and a 24 volt battery system) Vanner model 60-50A Abraham Solar.

BATTERY MAINTAINERS and DESULFATION

BATTERY WEB http://www.batteryweb.com/batterymindercomparison.cfm/ see this webpage for a run down on all the new battery maintenance technology. Never use a "trickle charger." Trickle chargers do not turn off and on to keep a float charge - they will overcharge the battery and ruin it eventually. Sulphation of the lead plates occurs on all batteries over time. There is one technology that keeps batteries from sulphating and one that can remove sulphation once it occurs.

SCHUMACHER SE-1125 Automatic Battery Charger/Maintainer (keeps battery at a perfect float charge without overcharging) about $25 from Wal-Mart and other auto parts stores.

DEEP DISCHARGE STORAGE BATTERIES
6-volt Golf Cart Batteries (about $49 each) cheap source (Costco Wholesale or Sam's Clubs).
Heavy Duty Deep Cycle Batteries for Solar Systems: Go to www.beselfreliant.com

DEKA BATTERS, see: Abraham Solar Tel: 800-222-7242.

TROJAN L-16 and L-16HC from Abraham Solar Tel: 800-222-7242.

AGM (absorbed Glass Matt) batteries. Heavy duty, high amperage delivery capacities without ruining battery. Optima or Lifeline batteries are 2 prominent brands. Check with Abraham Solar or an internet site like http://www.dcbattery.com/ .

USED SOLAR EQUIPMENT: www.abrahamsolar.com deals in lots of used solar equipment:

HYDROCAPS
These units condense the water vapor out of battery gassing so you don't have to water as often. Get them from Abraham Solar 1-800-222-7242.

HIGH SECURITY SHELTER

JUNCTION BOX
For solar array connections - contains SOV lightning arrestor. Model 53-911 from Abraham Solar.

WIRING SIZES (these will varying according to specific installation, but this should give you a general idea for a small to medium installation)
Solar Panels to J-Box #6 stranded copper.
J-Box to APT Power Center or Charge controller: (2) #2 stranded copper, 1 #6 stranded copper for external ground connection.
Battery interconnect cables #2 stranded copper (Abraham Solar) or auto supply stores.
Battery bank (last connection) to Inverter: #2/0 stranded copper, preferably welding wire.
Grounding cable: 1" wide braided copper.
12/24 VOLT FLUORESCENT LIGHTING

THINLITE Corp For 12 volt systems: use #197 (36" long) or #139 (48"long) fluorescent. For 24 volt systems use model numbers #297 or #239, same cost - about $65) from Abraham Solar or local RV supply stores carry Thinlite Products.

WHITE LED LIGHTS

WHITE LED FLASHLITE. Numerous brands available everywhere now.
18 LED SURFACE MOUNTING LIGHT "Super Nova" available in 12,24, 36, 48 volts.
Abraham Solar at 1-800-222-7242.
12v LIGHT BULBS local RV suppliers)
12 VOLT BATTERY CHARGER
Radio Shack, model 23-139

12 VOLT VENTILATION FANS
Best all-around choice is the DAYTON brand 12 volt fan from WW Grainger Stock # 2C646. About $46, 175 CFM and fairly quiet. A noisier, high rpm fan is by ITT JABSCO BRAND, also sold by W. W. GRAINGER, Stock # 4C814 (not for continuous duty - do not run more than 60 minutes at a time. This is an acceptable restriction as this fan will replace all the air in your shelter in less than 10-15 minutes). What makes these fans convenient is their 3" flange which allows you to easily attach it to the vent pipe shown in my shelter designs. The quieter DAYON fans need to have a flange adapter attached, which you can adapt from sheet metal duct parts available at most home improvement stores.

FUEL STORAGE EQUIPMENT

GASOLINE STABILIZER
Stabil, found at Pep Boys and other Auto Parts stores.
PRI: Proven #1 For Stability. This is the best stuff available. Use PRI-D & G to stabilize stored fuels. PRI-D & G can keep diesel fuel, kerosene, and gasoline fresh in storage. PRI-D & G can actually restore old fuels to refinery specifications. Yellowstone Trading: (800) 585-5077 URL: www.yellowstonetrading.com/ .

HIGH SECURITY SHELTER

OCTANE BOOSTER: Gives much better mileage on cars where timing is computer controlled to create maximum compression just short of knocking (most modern cars). It can be found at auto parts stores (helps rejuvenate old gasoline, so keep several bottles on hand for use with old stored fuel. Also keep fuel injector cleaners on hand to eliminate residues from old fuel) Cheapest at Wal-Mart.

DIESEL FUEL STORAGE ADDITIVE
Racor Biocide 1-800-344-3286. An insecticide plus additives to keep diesel fuel from growing algae and other solid organic matter. Call the 800 number to find distributor nearest you.
http://www.dieselpage.com/filter.htm/

FUEL TANKS (Available in all major cities. See Yellow Pages or check with local Petroleum distributor)

FUEL PUMPS (Check under Petroleum Equipment in Yellow pages)

FOOT VALVES Used at the bottom of a suction line. These are available at petroleum equipment dealers or at large plumbing outlets. Here are some sample brands of foot valves.
Simmons model 1402
Merril Series 810, model FV75
Water Ace model RFV75
Brady model SFV75 (plastic)

FOOD STORAGE
NOTES: Best buys in food storage are in bulk dried grains: Wheat, rice, and beans. Due to the shipping weight of bulk foods for storage, it best to buy these items close to home. (Shipping will cost you nearly $40/50 lb bucket, whereas if you can pick it up locally, you save those costs.) You can buy large bags of beans and rice at Costco and at Sam's Clubs nationwide. You can buy bulk wheat in many locations in the West, as indicated below. However, in the Midwest few grain growers bag any wheat for consumers. The best bet for people in the Midwest is to join together with a few other families and buy grain in bulk from the grower. Load up your pickup truck with grain, and then package it yourself plastic 6 gallon buckets. Many farmers in the Midwest and Canada have small grain cleaners that can take out the dust and other particles from field grain. Use a spoonful of diatomaceous earth per bucket of grain to kill any bugs.

DIATOMACIOUS EARTH
Sprinkle a tablespoon over and into a bucket of grain to kill all weevil. Harmless to humans. Available at any swimming pool supply house. It is used as a filter medium. It is also available at many garden stores since it is an effective pest control item (sprinkled on cabbage or lettuce, etc).

SOURCES OF DEHYDRATED FOODS AND PACKAGED GRAINS
Emergency Essentials Emergency Essentials 165 South Mountain Way Drive, Orem, UT 84058. Website: www.beprepared.com/ . Tel: 1-800-999-1863.
Provident Living: www.Providentliving.com
Montana Chemical Free Wheat Website: http://www.mtmarketplace.com/

Lehi Roller Mills Tripple-cleaned hard or soft wheat. Reasonable prices. Contact: (801) 768-4401, Address: 833 E. Main St., Lehi, Ut 84043. Website: http://www.lehirollermill.com/

HIGH SECURITY SHELTER

Walton Wheat Full service chemical free supply outlet for all types of survival foods and equipment. Very reputable. Contact: Walton Feed 135 North 10th, P.O. Box 307, Montpelier, ID 83254 Tel: 800-269-8563. Website: http://waltonfeed.com/

NON-HYBRID SEEDS
Territorial Seed Company P.O. Box 27, Lorane, Ore 97451 Tel: 541-942-9547.
Harris Seeds 1-800-514-4441.
Internet sources for hybrid seeds:
http://www.heirloomseeds.com/
http://www.organicseed.com/

WATER BARRELS
New 55 Gallon Polyethylene http://www.beprepared.com/

MOISTURE AND OXYGEN ABSORBERS (FOR DRY PACKING)
http://www.multisorb.com/

STORAGE BUCKETS
ROPAK WEST Tel 1-800-547-2347 (call to find distributor closest to you).

GENERATORS
SOURCES: Because of shipping weight, the heavier generators are sometimes best purchased from local generator dealers (see Yellow pages). However, always compare price with one of the major mail order generator supply houses. WW Grainger and Northern Tools will supply a wide variety of the cheaper or discontinued generator lines. For the best prices on the high quality units, call Norwall Power Systems Lake Havasu City, Az Tel: (520) 453-4494. Website: http://norwall.com/ These people ship all over the world and are experts - very good prices, too. They don't sell any junk, and service all major brands (so they know which ones are best for maintenance, too).

MINI PORTABLES
Small suitcase type gensets, less than 2000 watts, that are super quiet and super fuel-efficient:
Coleman Pulse 1850 (1.8kw) . Best buy of the quiet, small gensets that will run 7 hours day on 1.5 gal of fuel.
Yamaha EF1000 It is only 1kw but it is very fuel efficient and quiet and runs all day on a gallon of gas. Costs double the larger Coleman brand.
Honda EU1000i This is the newest high tech wonder from Honda, but it runs its current through a new high tech inverter - giving excellent sine wave power (but may be a high tech problem in maintenance - and also the most costly).

PORTABLES
There are two classes of generators here: the cheap group with flat-head, side valve, lawnmower type engines, and the more expensive group with longer life overhead cam and valve engines. Starting from the best and most expensive to the cheapest, lowest quality here is how I would rank them (from top to bottom):
Kawasaki GE Series Best maintenance history, rugged engines, pressurized oil system, great bearing surfaces - most expensive.

HIGH SECURITY SHELTER

Honda Deluxe Series Honda is one of those companies with a high quality line, and a medium quality line (the ECON models - don't confuse them).
Generac EXL Series Generac also has a high and low line. The XL or EXL lines have the pressurized oil system "vanguard" engine or the Honda engine.
Kubota AV Series - excellent machines (Kubota always builds nice engines).
Kubota Diesel Gensets Model GL6500 (6.5kw) about $4500 (Kubota Tractor Dealers).
Generac (cheaper lines)
Winco (cheaper lines)
Coleman Powermate 5kw gas generator - about $500 (cheapest, moderate quality, but most generator for the money).

STAND-BY GENERATORS
Top to bottom in price and quality:
Kohler simply the best in all regards, and most expensive. Rock solid engines and electronics. Kohler transfer switches rarely fail. Available in Gasoline, LP, NG (or all three) or Diesel.
Onan - second best overall, but some problems with electronic reliability in past) all fuels avail.
Hawk Power (Lester Petter diesel engines - English and Mitsubishi gas/lp/ng engines).
Generac II (8K and above are top quality engines) Best Buy for very good quality.
China Diesel Cheapest of the diesel gensets (buy a spare rebuild kit) and very noisy, but has a good reliability record. Recommend the 8000 Watt S195 Engine, 1800 RPM Brushless Alternator, Continuous Duty, Includes Radiator, This company now sells a full line of other standby and marine generators. Call 800-341-7027 or website: www.chinadiesel.com .

SPECIALTY STAND-BY
TRI-FUEL GENERATOR: For the ultimate in multi-fuel use, you can pay more and get a generator set up for three fuels: Gasoline, LP and NG. Onan or Kohler both have these units perfected. Call Norwall Power Systems, Lake Havasu City, Az Tel: (520) 453-4494.

STEAM ENGINES
TINY POWER: http://www.tinypower.com/
5 HP Liberty http://www.thesustainablevillage.com/servlet/display/product/detail/32104/
12 HP Steam GENSET http://www.thesustainablevillage.com/servlet/display/product/detail/30748/
Mike Brown Steam http://www.thesustainablevillage.com/servlet/display/product/detail/29811

BATTERY MAINTAINER
http://www.batteryweb.com/
Schaumacher Battery Maintainer, $25 from Wal-Mart stores, nationwide.

SPECIAL ACCESSORIES FOR GENERATORS
Manual and Auto Transfer Switches for Portable Generators:
Most Generator manufacturers offer a wide variety of these transfer switches. Abraham Solar is an expert on these.
Master Sales Website: http://www.mastersalesonline.com/ Call Toll Free 1-888-917-2244
SILENCING MUFFLERS FOR GENERATORS
HARCO, Inc Portland Oregon. (503) 244-7571. Website: www.harcomfg.com Harco has 2 levels of silencers: Super Critical (attenuates down to nearly silent) about $175, and Critical which is about $140.

They also have the same two levels in a "low Profile" unit for small, tight locations. These cost about 25-30% more. All these mufflers are stat-of-the-art silencers, and are very reasonably priced. You can afford to stack two mufflers together for super critical needs inside a home. Email at harco1@teleport.com.

HEATING EQUIPMENT

KEROSENE HEATERS
Kerosun DC 100 1-888-537-6786 Most fuel efficient and cleanest burn.

PROPANE WALL HEATERS (VENTLESS)
There are a variety of manufacturers of ventless heaters now. Most home improvement stores carry them. Vanguard is one brand. Another is:
Martin Industries, Florence Al website: www.martinindustries.com. model MIR12 (1-2 burner) MIR18 (1-3 burners) or MIR30 (1-6 burners) I prefer multiple small units spaced around the house for emergency LP gas heat. Also available in natural gas a "BEST BUY."

MULTI-FUEL FURNACES

TURBO HEAT MULTI-FUEL BOILER: Burns almost anything, can change burners http://www.beselfreliant.com/heating/index.cfm/
YUKON Multifuel Furnace (www.yukon-eagle.com) Alpha American Co.1000 Ag Science Drive, P.O. Box 20, Palisade, MN 56469 Tel: 1-800-358-0060.
CHARMASTER Products, Inc. http://www.charmaster.com 2307 No. 2 West Grand Rapids, Mn 55744 Tel: (218) 326-6768 (Makes combination wood/oil or gas furnaces and even a furnace with a fireplace front on the side.)

WOODSTOVES
Travis Industries, Inc. 10850 117th Place NE, Kirkland, WA 98033 Tel: (425) 827-9505 Makers of the LOPI high efficiency woodstoves, Avalon Pellet Stoves & Fireplace Xtrordinair lines of Wood, Pellet & Gas hearth heating stoves.
Avalon Wood stoves and Pellet Stoves Website: East coast: http://www.stoveworksnj.com/
Regency Wood Stoves and Gas Fireplaces. website: www.regency-fire.com . A highly recommended clean-burn stove without catalytic converter.

DIRECT VENT GAS/WOOD FIREPLACES
Heat-N-Glo Website: www.heatnglo.com. 20802 Kensington Blvd. Lakeville, MN 55044 Tel: 888-743-2887. Local dealers almost everywhere.
Regency Wood Stoves and Gas Fireplaces. website: www.regency-fire.com .

DEDICATED WOOD WATER HEATER
AquaHeater, LEHMAN'S item; #59-841; or Domestic Growers Supply (541) 592-3615.

COAL STOKER STOVES
Alaska Coal Stoker Pennwood Stoves, Fireplaces, Etc. West College Avenue, Pleasant Gap, Pa. 16823 Tel: 1-800-598-3995.

HIGH SECURITY SHELTER

AIR TO AIR HEAT EXCHANGERS
XeteX, Inc. 3530 E. 28th St. Minneapolis, MN 55406 Tel: (888) 899-9991 Toll Free or (612) 724-3101 voice mail. URL: www.xetexinc.com (This company has some of the best and most cost effective heat exchangers.)

HOUSEHOLD PREPAREDNESS EQUIPMENT

GENERAL INTERNET ORDER SOURCE
APPLIANCES ONLINE Website: www.appliances.com E-Mail: zupanci@ibm.net Voice & Fax: 440-543-8345. Good, one stop shopping for most small household appliances.

JUICERS
Champion Juicer: (about $215) from most health food stores.
Vita-Mix: About $360. Call 1-800-848-2649 for info.

KEROSENE STOVE
ALPACA (about $79) from Emergency Essentials.

WHOLE HOUSE HYPO-ALLERGENIC FILTERS SYSTEM
http://www.casadavida.com The CVI-series EnviroConditioner controls every parameter of indoor air quality. As an integrated part of the HVAC (heating, ventilation, air conditioning) system, the air in the entire house is processed and distributed through the central air conditioning ductwork. Nothing on the market can compare to the effectiveness of the CVI EnviroConditioner at any price. Very Pricey.
· Pressurizes the house with fresh outside air, exhausts stale air, and utilizes the structure of the building to create a hyberbaric chamber
· Advanced filtration remove over 99.7% of particulate matter from the air, eliminating dust in the house
· Sterilizes the airstream of virtually all biologicals, destroying viruses, bacteria, molds, mycobacteria, mildew, pollen, animal dander, dust mites, etc.
· Independent laboratory tests confirm the destruction of over 99.996% of viruses and over 99.999% of bacteria
· Eliminates environmental toxicants
· Eliminates odors- gives house a clean, fresh smell
· Eliminates smoke
· Destroys toxic mold

WHEAT/GRAIN GRINDERS-ELECTRIC/MANUAL
EVERYTHING KITCHENS: Online shopping of a full range of all the newest equipment:
http://www.everythingkitchens.com/grainmills.html
Grain Master "Whisper Mill" from Emergency Essentials or Waltons.
Magic Mill or K-Tec "Kitchen Mill" Same machine Same principle as Whisper mill but mill sits over canister - holds more flour, less complicated, a little less expensive. Same milling mechanism.
Golden Grain Grinder (conventional type of stone mill motorized grinder) Emergency Essentials.

MANUAL GRINDERS
Country Living Grain Mill http://www.countrylivinggrainmills.com/ V-groove wheel for quick and easy conversion to electric motor. Cast-iron flywheel for easy turning and smooth flow of flour. Large hopper

holds 2 lb. of wheat easy-Dial, self-locking adjustment. Double sealed industrial ball bearings. 30% less torque or energy required to turn than any comparable hand mill on the market. This grain mill is designed to be easily motorized. The fly wheel is grooved for use with a standard V Belt. We recommend using at least a 1/3 HP motor rated at 1150 RPM and equipped with a 1 1/2" pulley. This ratio will produce about 115 to 120 RPM at the flywheel. Other motors may be used, but they will need to be geared so that the RPM at the flywheel does not exceed 140 RPM.
The Family Grain Mill is unique in that it offers both a grain mill and a roller mill, as well as a choice of hand-powered or electric, or both. You can mix and match the components any way you want. Grain Mill with hand base or motorized base, Roller Mill with hand base or motorized base . Buy both on the hand base for about $196 from Homestead Products website http://www.homestead-products.com , phone in Oregon: 541-688-9263.

KITCHEN MIXERS
BOSCH Universal Kitchen System
K-TEC "Champ" Deluxe model with all attachments www.everythingkitchens.com/k-tecblender.html .
The Champ Mixer is the most versatile multi-function home food preparation machine available today. The Champ combines the features of a strong 1400 watt, 1.8 peak horsepower motor with a sophisticated, keypad-controlled computer "Bread Brain." The Champ computer assists the cook by measuring the resistance of the developing gluten in the bread and turns off the machine once it has developed perfectly. The Champ is also the strongest blender on the market. Our blender jar is made of GE Lexan plastic, the same material used in bullet-proof glass. The most popular attachment is the pasta maker/meat grinder combination.

PRESSURE CANNERS
All American is now producing the model 941 (41 quart) pressure canner. Smithfield Implement in Smithfield, UT has them in stock. If you need another source on home canning see http://www.home-canning.com/ . http://www.pressurecooker-outlet.com/americancans.htm/

PEELER
Apple, Potato Peeler (about $30, plus $12 for potato attachments) Emergency Essentials.
SMALL CONVENTIONAL REFRIGERATOR (most energy-efficient)
Magic Chef ct-1511AE (15 cubic ft) uses 1.2 kw/day $37/year.

LARGE CONVENTIONAL REFRIGERATOR (most energy-efficient)
Kitchen Aid, Whirpool, Kenmore 25 cu. ft. side-by-side use 1.75 kw/day or $54/year.

ALTERNATE ENERGY REFRIGERATORS
SUN FROST: www.abrahamsolar.com

SOLARFRIDGE: 19 cu. ft. (12 volt fridge) Better alternative to SunFrost but same high price. ($2,700) Simpler Solar 3118 W. Tharpe St.Tallahassee, FL 32303, website: www.simplersolar.com or call 1-800-248-9786. Two models of fridges use .5 and .7 kw/h for the 6 and 12 cu ft models.

KOOLATRON - small non compressor technology - about 2 cu. ft., 4 amp 12Vdc icebox. Available at outdoor stores.

Kool Mate 40 by Igloo. Another thermoelectric cooler like the Koolatron - sits upright or on its side so as to operate like a small fridge.

PROPANE OR KEROSENE REFRIGERATORS
NORCOLD: 2 way and 3-way 7.5 cu. ft. Propane fridge model 1082,
DOMETIC 7.5 cu. ft. propane fridge (same as Servel brand from Sweden) - about $1,200. Can also buy these with 120volt backup power, or in natural gas or kerosene. Most RV suppliers are Dometic distributors.

FOOD DEHYDRATORS
Magic Aire II On-Line Health Products 387 Yellowstone Ave., Pocatello, Idaho 83201 (800) 789-1577 or (208) 234-9352 http://www.dhi.com/ .
Air Preserve II On-Line Health Products 387 Yellowstone Ave., Pocatello, Idaho 83201 (800) 789-1577 or (208) 234-9352.
Harvest Maid (Available at many preparedness stores listed at the beginning.)

WATER DISTILLERS
Genesis 20-G3000 (about $250). This is a portable model, counter-top. Optimal Health Concepts 355 N. Lantana Street, Suite 730, Camarillo, CA 93010-9030. 24 hour Orders: 888-390-4676 http://intohealth.com/ This company sells a lot of excellent health products.

PORTABLE WATER FILTERS
PUREFLOW 2000 will remove bacteria, giardia, cryptosporidium, chlorine, chlorine byproducts, volatile organic compounds (VOCs), trihalomethanes, pesticides, herbicides, tastes, odors, and more. PureFlow 2000 purification starts with our highly efficient clean able ceramic microfilter which provides genuine sub-micron filtration. After all signs of bacteria and ultra fine sediment are removed, the PureFlow 2000 passes the water through a highly dense solid block of extruded activated carbon. Chlorine removal for 20,000 gallons (76,000 liters) of water at 1ppm chlorine. The PureFlow2000 "Plus" is the same System with a 3rd Filter for heavy debris URL: www.Supplies4Y2K.com/ Tel: (406) 375-9282 Mail: 610 N. 1st Street, Suite #5-150, Hamilton, MT 59840 USA.

BREAD MAKERS
Zojirushi V-20: order online from Costco for the best price about $145 www.costco.com. See a product review of all the bread makers at http://www.sonic.net/webpub/bread-machine/breadmachine.html

BREAD MIXERS
BOSCH mixer: This unit is the Cadillac of all combination units. There is no higher quality unit around. The unit with all the attachments, including everything imaginable, will run you several hundred dollars. Available at hundreds of online stores.

HIGH EFFICIENCY APPLIANCES WASHING MACHINES
Staber 2300 washing machine uses 1 oz., of soap, 21 gallons of water (saves 25 gallons/load), less than 200 watts per load. Spins faster, most of the water is removed. It is a top loader and the clothes go through a door in the rotating drum - not as convenient to load or unload because of the small opening. See Abraham Solar 1-800-222-7242.

HIGH SECURITY SHELTER

ASKO The best of the current models http://www.askousa.com/ Swedish import--top of the line Euro appliances. Also very high priced
MAYTAG Neptune Mod #MAH3000A. The matching Neptune dryer model MD3000A. Model number for Neptune Super Stack washer/dryer combo is MUE for electric dryer, and MUG for gas. Neptune washer uses 22 gallons of water per cycle instead of the old average amount of 38 gallons per cycle. Spin speed is 800 rpms on the old and 850 on the new. Because of the larger tub size on the Maytag Neptune, less rpms are required to extract the same amount of water as other brands. Use HE (high efficiency detergents) about $1,100.
FRIGIDAIRE (also Gibson) Front Loading Washer FT449GFS - spins up to 850 rpm dryer FSE748GF (matching front load). Low Price: $800 (best buy) also is a true under-counter model. Floor models can be stacked for convenience and without buying any extra cabinet.

MANUAL WRINGER WASHERS
The James Hand Washer is the washer of choice among those who wash by hand as a way of life. Its unique lever action makes agitating the clothes so easy a child can do it. It has a stainless steel tub and a wringer so efficient that it gets out twice as much moisture as spin drying. Very well-made and durable. Wringer can be bought separately for $130.00 The company that makes these will sell directly to you. Contact S & H Metal Products Inc., 122 Redman Dr, Topeka, IN (219) 593-2565. Or you can buy through Lehman's catalog,

MANUAL CLOTHES WRINGER
Buy a Chamois [chammy] wringer at auto supply stores for about $160 [Champ Catalogue item #J9-213] and mount on a 30 gal barrel. This is too high a price in my opinion. I would get the James washer wringer, instead. You can buy it directly from several other small outfits that carry them. Call the manufacturer, Lake City Industries at (814) 774-9616 to get a list of the nearest local source to you. It is called the #76-3 Hand Wringer.

PORTABLE COOK STOVES - KEROSENE
ALADDIN stoves carry the most complete line of kerosene heaters and stoves.
The ALPACA is great if you need something stronger and simpler than a backpacking stove. It's very sturdy and will take as large a pot as you care to put on it. Extremely simple, reliable design, with a minimum of moving parts to wear out. Fuel tank holds 0.9 gallons and has a fuel level gauge. Runs for 16 hours on a filling. Output 8,500 BTU; weight 13 lbs; size about 13" high x 13" diameter. There are many foreign models as well, since Europe and South America use kerosene extensively. PRIMUS is perhaps the largest foreign model.

WATERLESS COOKWARE
VOLLRATH: The heaviest and the best. The Vollrath Company, L.L.C., Tel: 1-800-624-2051, Fax: (920) 459-6570 website www.vollrathco.com .

LONG LASTING 130V LIGHT BULBS
FEIT ELECTRIC LA, CA lasts 14,000 hours and costs only a little more than standard bulbs - best buy on the market from home improvement stores.

COMPACT FLOURESCENTS
GE brand. They will run better off an inverter than other brands.

SUNPIPES
1,500 watts of free, fresh light as easy to install as stovepipe. Hollow, super-reflective pipe runs from your roof down to a translucent ceiling fixture that spreads the light down. Natural, full-spectrum light without glare, heat, or uncomfortable hot spots. Less expensive and easier to install than a skylight. Doesn't build up unwanted summer heat, create condensation, sun-fading problems, and won't leak.

KEROSENE LAMP AND PROPANE LANTERNS
Rapid Kerosene Pressure Lamp uses pressurized fuel and a mantle to generate 500 lumens (300 watt light bulb). Burns 10 hours from one-third gallon kerosene (one filling).
Petromax Multi-Fuel Lantern $120 from Homestead Supply. This German beauty is the Cadillac of lanterns. Burns all liquid fuels, nickel finish, very classy. Puts out tremendous light. See: www.petromax.com
Dietz Wick-Oil Lamp The best of the old fashioned wick/oil lamps - beautiful and inexpensive. Lanterns Online, http://members.tripod.com/~timcallen/lantern/index.htm .
Humphrey Propane Lamps The oldest and best company
http://www.thesustainablevillage.com/servlet/display/products/byCat/7/29/170

FULL SPECTRUM COMPACT FLUORESCENT
Sun-A-Lite Compact fluorescent replace screw-in bulbs with total spectrum, radiation-shielded fixtures.
Excella Full spectrum fluorescents 20 watts to 40 watt tubes
All home improvement stores now sell full spectrum fluorescents now.

FEATHER QUILTS, BEDS
The Company Store: http://www.thecompanystore.com/ 500 Company Store Rd, LaCrosse WI 54601, Tel: 1-800-356-9367.

RESIDENTIAL ELEVATORS
Lift-Avator 435 Park Ave, Lockport, NY 14094 Tel: (716) 434-1300. URL: http://www.stair-ease.com/
Tri-State Elevators at http://www.tri-state-lift.com shows 4 or 5 of the most common residential elevators.
Tri State Lift 1414 South Oak Street Owatonna, MN 55060 Toll Free Call: 1-800-626-6017.

NUCLEAR PROTECTION EQUIPMENT

RADIATION METER
Victoreen 717 surplus survey meters. Range 0-500 rads, comes with detachable ion chamber so you don't have to buy a separate probe to take measurements outside the shelter. Uses 1 "D-Cell" battery. Simple, low tech, reliable. These are not in production, unused in new condition. Have not been calibrated since production. Calibration will usually drift 10-20% at the most, which is not critical for the high dose measurements you would make in a nuclear war. KI4U website: http://www.radmeters4u.com/

CALIBRATION NOTE: Meters can be recalibrated if necessary by sending them to KI4U.com or Jordan Nuclear, 3244 Arroyo Seco Ave, L.A. CA 90065. Call for rates: 1-(323) 222-8143. Mgr: Ed Manughian
Dosimeter Corporation model 3510. Range 0-3000 rads. Probe is extra. Top of the line quality. Contact Tel: 1-800-322-8258.
KFM kit meter (Under $20) order from Emergency Essentials, Orem Utah. (1-800-999-1863).

HIGH SECURITY SHELTER

NUCLEAR BIOLOGICAL, CHEMICAL (NBC) FILTER SYSTEM
Model LUWA 180, about $6,000 - super expensive. US Rep. for the Swiss Luwa Corporation is Sharon Packer, Utah Shelter Systems, PO Box 638, Heber, Ut 84032 or on the web: http://www.disastershelters.net/

MILITARY NBC ROOM FILTER
This unit is US made for the military and much cheaper than the LUWA. More importantly, it can be mounted outside your shelter where the particles trapped in the filter won't radiate your shelter.
HUNTER MFG: http://www.huntermfgco.com/homedef/protectivefiltrationHF100C.htm/
Model HF100C 100-cfm NBC Filter Canister Price: less than $2,000 Features: 100-cfm airflow Self-contained canister ASZM-TEDA carbon media Modularity allows for multiple filter applications Horizontal or vertical installation The HF100C is the civilian version of the US Army M48A1 100 cfm gas and particulate filter canister manufactured by Hunter.

ALTERNATE AND CHEAPER NBC FILTERS (HEPA SPECS)--for light duty
Order all 3 Replacement filters for a Honeywell "Enviracaire" model #63200 filter unit:
1. Replacement HEPA filter (down to 3 microns) (#28600) about $90
2. Replacement CPZ filter (#36200) about $90
3. Replacement charcoal Pre-filters (pkg of 2) - (#34002) $20
WW GRAINGER carries the HEPA and the CPZ filter, but not the charcoal pre-filters. Here are the Grainger stock numbers: HEPA FILTER: 3GD14, CPZ FILTER: 3GD18

12 VOLT FANS
ITT JABSCO, model 35115-0020
WW GRAINGER stock # 4C814 Note, these are plastic blowers, high RPM 4200, hence noisy. These are not meant to be run on continuous duty (for continuous duty fan, order stock #2C646a 12 volt, 176 CFM). 110volt fan (141 cfm) for ventilation under normal power, buy unit number 2C916.
Round AUTO AIR FILTERS to place over shelter air inlets, about $5 each. available at auto supply stores.

EMP PROTECTION
EMP PROTECTORS
Zero Surge: The newest instantaneous clamping technology. Use for all your valuable plug in products like computers. ZeroSurge 944 State Route 12, Frenchtown, NJ 08825 Tel: 800-996-6696 Email: sales@zerosurge.com URL: www.zerosurge.com .
Alpha Delta Communications P.O. Box 620, Manchester, KY 40962 Tel. 606-598-2029 Products: Coax lightning arrestors, coax switches with surge protectors. http://www.alphadeltacom.com/
Ameritron, Louisville Road Starkville, MS 39759 Tel. 601-323-8211 Products: Remote coax switches, inrush AC current protector. http://www.ameritron.com/
ICE: Industrial Communication Engineers, Ltd. Website: http://www.iceradioproducts.com/ P.O. Box 18495, Indianapolis, IN 46218-0495 Tel. 317-545-5412 Products: Coax lightning arrestors suitable for EMP.
Polyphaser Corp. P.O. Box 9000, Minden, NV 89423-9000 Tel. 702-782-2511 Products: top of the line military grade EMP protection equipment. Prime source of all US government equipment, but expensive. Check with ICE first.

HIGH SECURITY SHELTER

GROUNDING STRAPS, ETC

Certified Quality (The WIREMAN : http://thewireman.com/index.shtml) 261 Pittman Rd., Landrum, SC 29356 Tel. 800-727-9473 (orders), 803-895-4195 (Tech line) Products: The Wireman stocks copper wire up to #4 AWG, 2-inch flat copper strap, 8-foot copper-clad ground rod and 1 x 1/4 inch bus bar.
Rohn Towers P.O. Box 2000, Peoria, IL 61656 Tel. 309-697-5612 Products: Radio towers mostly, but also copper strap and tower grounding products. Rohn products available through Amateur Electronic Supply or Ham Radio Outlet (listed in radio section)

FALLOUT SHELTERS

PREFAB CONCRETE TANKS (use for burial underground)

Oldcastle Precast (Custom precast waterproof concrete tanks - Address: 2820 A Street, SE, Auburn, WA 98071-0608 Tel: (253) 833-2777 Fax: (253) 939-9126 Website: www.oldcastle-precast.com Toll free: (888) 232-6274. They have local manufacturers all over the USA.

UNDERGROUND STEEL TANK-TYPE FALLOUT SHELTER (using 8' round steel culvert pipe--about $10,000 to build)

Utah Shelter Systems P.O. Box 638,-Heber, Ut 84032 (Sharon Packer (801) 942-5638). http://www.disastershelters.net/
Storm Chaser Shelters http://www.stormandtornado.com/ 1200 Lawson Road, Fort Worth, TX 76131 Tel: (817) 847-9000.
Do-It-Yourself Plans for tank type shelters from Art Robinson, Oregon Institute of Science and Medicine, 2251 Dick George Road, Cave Junction, Oregon 97523 Tel: (541) 592-4142.

BASEMENT FALLOUT, SECURITY SHELTERS

see "The Secure Home" by Joel Skousen URL: www.joelskousen.com/

CONCRETE BLOCK SHELTERS with stack block roof, built into existing homes - see "How To Implement A High Security Shelter in the Home" by Skousen, http://www.joelskousen.com/Secure/reports.html#HS/

STEEL PLATE SHELTERS, CUSTOM OR PREFAB

SAFECASTLE http://www.safecastle.com/home.php/

CO2 MONITOR

Tells you if carbon dioxide from occupant breathing activity is getting too high. Elevated CO_2 will cause problems before you run out of oxygen. This unit also senses Oxygen levels too: Industrial Scientific, model CMX271. About $1200, $600 used or repaired. http://www.plccenter.com/buy/Industrial+Scientific/CMX27

DRY FLUSH PORTABLE TOILET

Porta-John Systems, Inc. A Waterless Toilet. This portable, free-standing toilet doesn't use any water, but dry suctions everything into a bottom compartment lined with a plastic garbage bag. After 30 flushes, simply remove bag. http://www.toilets.com/products/waterless.htm

ELECTROSTATIC CARPET SWEEPER

HIGH SECURITY SHELTER

FULLER BRUSH sales Item # 101 - Price $49.99. Check with your local Fuller Brush salesperson. Many have internet sites such as http://www.hfbd.com/

PLUMBING SYSTEMS

COMPOSTING TOILETS
BIOLET mini-composting toilet. Finally a composter about the size of a regular toilet! www.biolet.com Tel: 1-800-5biolet (US) 800-6biolet (Canada)
CLIVUS MULTRUM II for large unified system, using special toilets. Will compost continuous use for multiple people and also kitchen waste. Large size, must be sited in a basement area.
SUN-MAR CENTREX PLUS moderately small sized for placement in bathroom. Works on AC or DC power, automatic controls available. From $1,200-1,800 depending on options.

GREYWATER SYSTEM
EARTHSTAR Grey water Systems Automatic operation, sand filter with backwash cleaning. Available at Sustainable Village: http://www.thesustainablevillage.com/servlet/display/product/detail/28514

GREYWATER FILTER
Filter and tank, with DC or AC pump Sustainable Village, see above.
BIODEGRADABLE LAUNDRY DETERGENT - must use with grey water so as not to damage plants. Real Goods http://www.gaiam.com/

SANITATION EQUIPMENT
Chemical Toilets: ($20-50) available at camping and RV stores.
Marine Toilets: --My preferred manual toilet recommendation for shelters. These toilets have a manual pump that will pump waste up a 1-1/2" pipe as high as 6' allowing use in basement shelter systems where one must connect to existing plumbing drains at ceiling height. JABSCO brand, call 1-714-545-8251 to find distributor nearest you. Available at yacht and marine supply stores - order model #29120-2000 for the larger, elongated bowl.
Dry Flush Toilet: Porta-John® Systems, Inc. 50633 Ryan Road, Utica, Michigan 48317
Tel: 1-888-PORTA-JOHN (1-888-767-8256).

POTASSIUM IODATE TABLETS Take after any nuclear incident to avoid thyroid contamination by radioactive iodine uptake. www.KI4U.com

HYDRAULIC RAMS
Here's an explanation of how they work: http://www.p2pays.org/ref/01/00971.htm
Columbia Hydraulic Ram contact: Skookum Co. Inc. 8524 N. Crawford St. Portland, OR 97203.
Pacific Hydro Corp. 400 Forbes Blvd. San Francisco, CA 94080
Rife Hydraulic Engine Mfg. Co. 316 W. Poplar St., P.O. Box 790, Norristown, PA 19401 Tel: (717) 740-1100 Fax: (717) 740-1101 Email: rife@epix.net/
Highlifter Pumps and B & L Hydraulic Rams (cheaper and simpler) from Abraham Solar Equipment.

HIGH EFFICIENCY CONVENTIONAL WATER HEATERS
Vaughn Manufacturing Corporation, 26 Old Elm St., P.O. Box 5431, Salisbury, MA 01952-5431 Tel: (978) 462-6683 (R-18 Urethane insulated, hydrastone-sealed tanks for long life).

HIGH SECURITY SHELTER

Rheem/Rudd -Marathon Non Metalic tank - should last a lifetime. Electric only. (available from all Rheem/Ruud dealers) R-20 urethane insulation. The Imperial Plus line of standard water heaters are 10 year warranty R-20 units) see URL: www.rheem.com/ .

WOOD WATER HEATERS

AquaHeater Lehman's also sells a stand-alone water heater (their "System Two" unit) which is an AquaHeater that heats hot water in only 12 minutes without electricity! It provides a continuous supply as long as the fire is maintained. After the fire goes out, the insulated tank keeps the 10 gallons of water hot for hours. It produces up to two gallons of water per minute. http://www.lehmans.com/

LOW SURGE SUBMERSIBLE WELL PUMPS

Grundfos Variable Speed 3 inch submersible pump. Check www.us.grundfos.com .

12 OR 24 VOLT SOLAR CIRCULATION PUMPS

Grundfos: www.us.grundfos.com Available through most plumbing distributors.

FLEXIBLE PLASTIC PIPING AND MANIFOLDS

There is no better plumbing system for the do-it-yourself plumber than plastic pipe systems. You used to have two choices. One was polybutylene. It is very flexible and freeze resistant since it will expand rather than split or break. There has been a lot of bad press given to polybutylene due to the occurrence of leaks in the older systems (almost always at joints with plastic fittings that cracked under improper clamping). This pipe will soon be replaced by the following improved version:

POLYETHYLENE PIPE (PEX)

This is the newest type of plastic pipe that is on the market. It appears to be stronger and more chemical and heat-resistant than polybutylene. It also uses the new manifold type plumbing junction connections like polybutylene. It is a little more expensive, however. See URL www.vanguardpipe.com for details. Available at all plumbing supply stores.

WATER TANKS

There are several types of plastic water tanks on the market - all of them preferable to steel in the small to medium sizes. The white tanks are POLYPROPYLENE, colored tanks are usually POLYETHYLENE, and black tanks are ABS plastic. FIBERGLASS tanks are used for the larger reinforced tanks and are not suitable for stored drinking water due to chemical out gassing. I will not list individual suppliers here because these are obtained locally in every rural farm community in the country, including the entire East Coast. Check the Yellow Pages for "tanks" or "water tanks."

Kolaps A Tank (bladder type collapsible tank, useful for hauling water in a pickup, and for temporary storage. It will even act as a giant solar water heater. http://www.burchkolaps-a-tank.com/

RADIO EQUIPMENT

All of the following equipment is available from Ham Radio Outlet or AES - the two biggest mail order radio stores - contact info at beginning of section.

FAMILY BAND RADIO

No license required, 1-2 mile range, low powered - like a walkie talkie, only higher quality. Available at electronic and radio stores locally--these are the best buy alternatives in radio. Best deals at Costco

HIGH SECURITY SHELTER

CB RADIO
40 Channel: Radio Shack (NO LICENSE REQUIRED).

SHORT WAVE RECEIVERS Portable
Sony ICF-SW100s The ultimate in miniature-sized world band receiver (size of cassette)
Grundig Satellite 700 best sound of the high-end, full sized portables.
Sony ICF-SW7600G Best buy of the medium-sized, fully capable receivers.
Note: I do not recommend the Baygen (Freeway brand) wind-up radio, unless you must have the wind-up option. The radio receiver is not a high quality unit compared to those listed above. Even the sub-$100 name brand SW radios are superior.

HF TRANSCEIVERS (transmit and receive; compact and portable} - MUST HAVE HAM LICENSE. The 4 major manufacturers, Yaesu, Icom, Kenwood, and Standard all put out extremely high quality products. Each have a similar range. If you aren't going to get deep into ham radio (which requires a lot of study and time), choose an HF transceiver that has the minimum features plus a built-in antenna tuner. These will cost between $1,200-$2,000. Don't go for the top of the line models as they are very complex and hard to remember how to use.
Kenwood TX-50S 12 volt Portable: can be mounted in a vehicle.
Kenwood TS-850S/AT Desktop model: built in antenna tuner.
UHF, VHF radios, portable base station, dual band, plus capable of acting as a repeater
Kenwood TM733 (2m/440mhz)

HANDHELD PORTABLE
(2m/440mhz) Kenwood TH-79A

ANTENNAS
Car mount: Diamond NR-72BNMO, base station Diamond X-200A.
CB antennas, car mount. Radio Shack.
MOBILE HF ant: Outbacker Perth. Vertical Home base ant: Cushcraft R7.
Short Wave Antenna for your portable: SWL antenna , Ham Radio Outlet.

SCANNERS
Hand held, continuous coverage: AOR AR1000XLT .
Desk top: Bearcat 8500XLT 500 channels, not continuous coverage of all frequencies.
Antenna for Scanners: Home base station: Diamond D130.

SECURITY EQUIPMENT

SPECIALTY METAL HATCH DOORS The biggest and best company to supply all types of specialty hatch doors (roof, floor, and wall hatches) is Bilco door - long known for their sloping basement/tornado shelter doors. URL: www.bilco.com/ The Bilco Company, P.O. Box 1203, New Haven, Connecticut 06505 Tel: 203-934-6363.

WINDOW WELL SECURITY
The Improvement Network (www.windowwell.com) markets a full range of lexan plastic window well covers for emergency escape and security against entry. Tel: 888/934-6776.

HIGH SECURITY SHELTER

HURRICANE RESISTANT WINDOWS

Jarrett, Inc, Full range of custom hurricane-proof windows made to order, set in traditional window frames. http://www.jarrett-windows.com/Other-Specialties.htm 1-800-533-5097 .

PROTECTIVE FILM

Shatterguard Unbreakable backing to standard glass - can be applied to existing windows. Makes windows bullet-proof to small caliber (.22) weapons and makes windows impenetrable to intruders. www.shattergard.com. You can also use this on car side and rear windows to keep thieves from breaking in, which is highly recommend. http://www.shatterguard.com/wellsfargo.html

STEEL UTILITY DOORS:

SteelCraft. This company makes the heaviest gauge production doors available. You can get both B14 doors and 14 gauge frames which are bullet-resistant to some small .22 or 25 caliber arms. This is the door I spec for my gravel fill option, with two deadbolts for providing the least expensive secure door for a shelter. It is bullet proof for all normal handgun loads. To order the lock prep option, specify opt. 161. Contact: SteelCraft 9017 Blue Ash Road, Cincinnati, OH 45242 Tel: (513) 745-6400 or Toll Free: (800) 243-9780

VAULT DOORS

Homeland Security Safe Company: has an economy vault door for about $1500. see: http://www.homelandsafes.com/economyVaultDoor.php

Liberty Safe Co. Springville, Utah Tel: (801) 489 8550. They have local dealers around the country. These are for high security doors on safe rooms. See may High Security Shelter report (appendix) for installation details. About $3-4000.

LIGHT WEIGHT VAULT DOOR for retrofit onto a closet or security room:

AMSEC Model VD8030 Door opening: 77-1/2" H x 26-1/2"W Weight: 550 lbs. American Security Products Co. 11925 Pacific Avenue Fontana, CA 92337 Tel: 1-800-421-6142.

BULLET-PROOF DOOR

Amweld series 1544, bullet resistant to Level 3 (high powered handguns) about $1,500 including high security locks. Amweld Building Products, Inc.,1500 Amweld Drive Garrettsville, Ohio 44231 Email: info@amweld.com Tel: 1.330.527.4385. Http://www.amweld.com

Trussbilt level III and level IV ballistic protection available. Trussbilt's detention hollow metal products are used in prisons, jails, juvenile facilities and detention centers worldwide. http://www.trussbilt.com/html/detenholmetoverview.htm

ARMORED STEEL PLATE

Custom ordered for door sized 5/16" tempered steel - level 4 protection - 7.62 high velocity military rounds). Order from Heflin Steel Phoenix, Az Tel: 1-800-528-4021 or local 252-8061. Attach this plate to a SteelCraft Series B-14 door with pour-in-place F-14 steel frame (for 8" concrete. If you are near a large city in the East, call around to see if any steel distributors carried tempered steel or armored steel plate.

SECURITY CLOSET DOOR

Total Door http://www.totaldoor.com/DesktopDefault.aspx

HIGH SECURITY SHELTER

BULLET-PROOF PANELS
(Kevlar fiber building panels for protecting walls) .
BULLDOG DIRECT: http://www.bulldogdirect.com/directory-frame.html
ARMORCO http://www.armorco.com/shop/item.asp?itemid=242

KEVLAR REINFORCING PANELS AND WEBBING FOR HOMES
"GlasArmor" panels are $357.00 each for a 4' x 8' size FOB Birmingham, AL. contact: Steve Murphy Glasforms Inc. 8100 Banks Mill Road, Douglasville, GA 30135
Tel 770-489-9620 Cell 256-689-1321

4X8 KEVLAR/FIBER PANELS. Use webbing to create an earthquake or tornado-proof room or closet in the home. Nail special Kevlar webbing crosswise (X-pattern) around home or walls to make powerfully rigid shear walls. Also binds home down to foundation. Tape is 3" wide in 100 foot rolls and about the thickness of a nickel. --Very strong stuff.
New Necessities 5710 Pebblebrook Trail Gainesville, GA 30506 Tel: 770-844 URL: www.millibar.com. (Currently, 2006, it doesn't look like they are doing business). Use Spectra Shield by Bulldog Direct, above

BULLET-PROOF FABRICS, VESTS
BulletProofME.com (Nick Taylor) Brand-name bullet proof vests and body armor accessories at discounted prices. Very reliable source you can trust. URL: http://www.BulletProofME.com .
Bulldog Direct P.O. Box 8561 Cincinnati, Ohio 45208-8561 Tel: (513) 281-6700 Website: http://bulldogdirect.com .

BULLETS:
http://www.cheaperthandirt.com/ammo.asp

SPOTTING SCOPES, TELESCOPES
For a great place to buy binoculars, spotting scopes, telescopes, and accessories, try Eagle Optics at www.eagleoptics.com or call 1-800-289-1132

SOUND PROOFING FINGER FOAM (for Underground Shooting Ranges)
SONEX by Ilbruck Inc, 3800 Washington Ave North Minneapolis, Mn 55412. Tel (612) 521-3555. Website: http://www.sonexfoam.com/

GATE OPENERS
The latest technology uses hydraulic actuators instead of gear motors.
STANLEY full range of residential and commercial gates and opening types (available nationwide) call 1-800-STANLEY for distributor info.
Mighty-Mule Gate Openers: GTO Inc. 738 Capital Circle NW, Tallahassee, Fl. 32304 Tel: 1-800-543-4283.

ROLLING SECURITY SHUTTERS
ALL SEASON ROLLING SHUTTERS: These people have the best product on the market now.
http://www.allseasonshutters.com/

HIGH SECURITY SHELTER

Roll-A-Way offers rolling or accordian shutters in Aluminum, PVC, or clear Lexan. email: info@roll-a-way.com Rollaway National Headquarters 10601 Oak Street NE, St. Petersburg, FL 33716 Tel: (800) 683-3230 (888) ROLLAWAY.
Rolsafe URL: www.rolsafe.com/ 5845 Corporation Circle Fort Myers, FL, 33905 Tel: (941) 694-5400 Fax: (941) 694-8000 Toll Free: 1 800 833-5486
Rolladen: Top of the line, most expensive system, aluminum, PVC rolling shutters. Rolladen also produces working colonial security shutters. Tel: (800) 748-8837.

SECURITY SYSTEMS
GE SECURITY PRO:
Security Pro 6000 (Another ITI company for wireless or hardwired connections) URL: http://www.gesecuritypro.com/NorthAmerica/residential/product.cfm?ProdID=5&ptID=1 .
The Security Pro® 6000 can deliver as much security as you want. It starts out as an attractive entry-level system, but its unique design lets you upgrade it easily--at your pace--so you never have to pay for more system than you want. Add powerful options like wireless sensors that check their own operation so you always know whether the system is working properly. Add light control for added security and convenience. Add telephone control for remote operation, audio verification for false-alarm prevention. Add the peace of mind of numeric paging in emergencies and you'll see what makes the Pro 6000 one of the most valuable additions to any home or business.

HONEYWELL: Used to be APEX (hardwired) Advantage has the latest in voice prompting technology (voice tells you where intrusion is). It also has numerous control features included which allow you to control lights and equipment automatically. See the 6100 or 6100-wt Security panels at URL http://www.security.honeywell.com/hsce/products/control/bu/ap/11796.html .

ADT Pro Custom: (hardwired or wireless) ADT is the largest national chain of alarm systems. The ProCustom system has most of the features that the Honeywell/Apex system has, including voice annunciation and being able to check the whole house from any master keypad. 1-800-238-3009 or www.adt.com. Check out the entire listing and description of all the different types of security devices you can order: http://www.adt.com/resi/products-services/browse-system-components/component/?subCategory=71&categoryId=71

RETARDANT SPRAY
Sprays for shingles, wood siding, cardboard - almost everything. Water-based, non-toxic, safe.
Flame Stop: http://flamestop.com/?source=google
Cold Fire: http://middlebury.net/coldfire/
Flame Seal Products Inc. 4025 Willowbend Blvd. #310, Houston, TX 77025 Tel: 713 668 4291 URL: www.flameseal.com .

SECURITY COMPONENTS, MAIL ORDER
Mountain West Supply Co. 9405 E. Doubletree Ranch Road, #B234, Scottsdale, AZ 85258 local Tel: 602-971-1200 Toll Free: 1-800-528-6169.
Security Base.com www.securitybase.com .

INTERCOMS with Cameras

HIGH SECURITY SHELTER

NUTONE get their top of the line unit, with remote listen in, plus up to 10 cameras. http://www.nutone.com/product-category.asp?CategoryID=701

VEHICLE ALARM SYSTEM Add-on type
Mobile Alert Vehicle Security System: Radio Shack.
Optima II (monitors vehicle electric system for any turn on, or motion) from a variety of online sources. Sample: http://www.guarddog.net/aalarm.htm .

HIDDEN VIDEO CAMERAS
Security Base Phone: 1-800-616-0213 URL: www.securitybase.com (has the widest selection of covert video cameras. Look under "CCTV").

VIDEO MOTION DETECTION
Quark manufactures a complete line of Video Motion Detectors, from lower resolution (generally indoor use) 8, 12, and 18 channel devices (the Q-line) to enhanced 4 & 8-channel unit (the ESP-line) to the NET-line of 4 & 8 channel high resolution devices. URL: www.quarkdigital.com 1 800 327 5616.

DTS-1000 A more expensive commercial lineup of equipment to allow computers to detection intrusion and motion from a video surveillance camera. Website: http://www.magal-ssl.com/products/?pid=22

MICROWAVE FENCE AND PERIMETER DETECTION
SouthWest Microwave http://www.southwestmicrowave.com , Tempe, Arizona. INTREPID system - uses coax cable and sensor to detect any vibration (3 yards accuracy) on fence from climbing. Their MICRONET system is even more accurate and displays to a computer screen with map of your property layout.

SAFES
LIBERTY SAFE CO Builds gun safes and vault doors for home installation. Springville, Utah (801) 489 8550 (also builds National and Remington brand safes). http://www.libertysafe.com/

FLOOR SAFES
Hayman Safes (Website: www.haymansafe.com)
Adesco Floor Safes (Website www.adesco.com)

SURVEILLANCE AND ANTI-SURVELLANCE EQUIPMENT:
Electromax International Inc. 11140 Westheimer, #276, Houston, Texas 77042 Tel: (281) 531-7437. Check out the full range of high-tech equipment available for surveillance and for counter-surveillance work. http://www.electromax.com/indexreg.html .

DRIVEWAY MONITORS
DWA-3 Suitable for burying beside driveway - so you won't have to dig up asphalt or concrete drive. ($200) URL: www.drivewayalarms.com .

GARAGE DOOR OPENER ENCRYPTION
These systems rotate the codes on your door openers so they cannot be reused by a burglar who uses a special electronic eavesdropper to record your code. All new garage door openers come with this system

HIGH SECURITY SHELTER

built-in. Code Encrypter Plus, or Code Encrypter II, by RCI Automation, (619) 484-6307 URL: http://ourworld.compuserve.com/homepages/rciautomation/p4.htm .

STRESS FLOOR DETECTORS
Pressure sensors for use under flooring or roofs or under decks of boats for marine security. PULSORS (8000 series) by Sure Action, Inc URL: www.sureaction.com .

GPS VEHICLE LOCATORS
To protect against auto theft or carjacking and kidnapping in your own vehicle. Small transmitter is hidden in vehicle which allows a GPS signal to alert a North American tracking company of the vehicle location.
Aertrax Vehicle Locator Address: AerComTec International, 1359 Silver Bluff Rd., Suite G-5, Aiken, South Carolina 29803 Tel: (803) 649-2900. Available from many sites online: Sample: http://www.spysupplystore.com/aertrax.html

ROOM FOGGER
Smoke Cloak fogs the room in seconds with a dense, non-toxic glycerin-based fog that dissipates with no residue. This is an excellent passive defense against mobs or vandals entering the home. Smokecloak Ltd., 10 Cochran Close, Crownhill, Milton Keynes, MK8 0AJ, ENGLAND Phone : 44 (0) 1908 567007 URL www.smokecloak.com Email: sales@smokecloak.com.

HIGH SECURITY DEAD BOLTS
Medeco: Has special pins and key that rotates the lock tumbler pins to prevent picking
URL: www.medeco.com (Available at Locksmiths everywhere).
Assa 6000 pickproof, double-keyed, drill resistant deadbolt (at locksmiths nationwide).

ELECTRIC DOOR STRIKES
Von Duprin Company, Strike Force electric latches. http://www.vonduprin.com/prod-strikeforce.asp

BRONZE PIVOT BEARINGS
For concealed pivoting cabinet (about $3 for a set of two). All major cities have bearing specialty shops. Check the phone book. Ask for oil-impregnated brass or bronze bushings.

ARMORED CAR CONVERSIONS
Alpine Armoring Inc. 503 Carlisle Drive, Herndon, Virginia 20170 Tel: 703-471-0002 or 1-800-992-7667 http://www.alpineco.com/armored/vehicles.htm .
Bulldog Direct: Your do-it-yourself source. Armored Vehicle Kits. Armored vehicle kits provide N.I.J. level IIIA hand gun protection from: 9 mm, .357 mag., .44 mag., and higher. Each armor kit comes with installation instructions. Bulldog Direct, P.O. Box 8561, Cincinnati, Ohio, U.S.A., 45208-8561 Tel: (513) -281-6700
URL: www.bulldogdirect.com .

PRIVATE ENCRYPTION SOFTWARE FOR COMPUTERS
Pretty Good Privacy (PGP) Learn all about it from URL: www.pgp.com.

HEARING AMPLIFICATION MUFFS

HIGH SECURITY SHELTER

WOLF EARS: These specialty ear muffs will not only amplify small sounds, but they will attenuate loud sounds so that everything comes within your hearing comfort range. These are a must for combat shooting when you want ear protection but not so much as to keep you from detecting intrusions. These are very high tech. Here is the online source list: http://www.derry.gentexcorp.com/hearing-resellers.htm

SOLAR EQUIPMENT
For complete installation of full system, contact www.beselfreliant.com or www.abrahamsolar.com

PHOTOVOLTAIC SOLAR PANELS
Abraham Solar 1-800-222-7242. New and Used.

POLE MOUNTED SUN TRACKING EQUIPMENT (OPTIONAL)
Wattsun Sun Tracker (for a pole-mounted, tilting rack for solar panels to track sun) Abraham Solar 800-222-7242.
Zomeworks pole mount trackers, P.O. Box, Albuquerque, NM 25805, Telephone: (505) 242-5354 also from Abraham Solar 800-222-7242.

ROOF MOUNTED PANEL RACKS (rotating racks for roof mounting)
Zomeworks Albuquerque NM P.O. Box 25805, Tel: (505) 242-5354 or Abraham Solar.
A. For slanted roof mount: Order 2 drive axles, and one slave axle.
B. For Pole mount, 12 panels. Order 8612 unit - rack only, not the sun tracker.
Direct Power Fixed rack for direct roof mount: (2) six panel racks from Abraham Solar.

SOLAR CHARGE CONTROLLERS
When not using the more expensive XANTREX/TRACE power center option, try the following alternatives from Abraham Solar 800-222-7242.
A. Sun Selector NDR-30 CD-EMP(30 amp capacity with power divert). There are other models available depending on system size.
B. Sun Selector M-16 (16 amp capacity with no automatic power diversion) for small systems.

SOLAR WATER PUMPS from Abraham Solar
Coenergy and Aerovironment provide turn-key pumping systems. Check with Mick Abraham and Abraham solar. 800-222-7242
Individual pumps as follows:
SolarJack SCS Submersible Centrifugal Pumps - expensive submersibles down to 800 feet deep, performance comparable to small conventional pumps.
Powerlifter 1000
Shurflow or Flowjet pumps for lower cost pumps.
Slowpumps are medium-priced pumps that pump high vertical distances with low power, and low, steady output. Good for domestic water.
Dankoff Solar Surface Pumps - non-submersible centrifugal pumps for irrigation, using a small length of suction hose to draw from a creek or pond.
Highlifter Ram type pump. Use where you have no power source other than a stream. Will pump water between 400 and 1,000 high, depending on model. Volume is low, but steady. Very reliable.

SOLAR DESALINATORS

HIGH SECURITY SHELTER

AGUA DEL SOL Agua Del Sol, PO Box 1114, Pima, AZ 85543 Tel: (520) 485-9211 (www.mrsolar.com) Prices: $650-$850 output 1-3 gallons per day (panels 4, 6, or 8 ft long x 36" wide).
PUR (Recovery Engineering) Models: Survivor 35 (manual).2115 (smaller life raft model), PowerSurvivor 40E, Recovery Engineering, Inc. 2229 Edgewood Ave. S., Minneapolis, MN 55426 Tel: 800-845-7873 local: 612-541-1313. Sample seller:
http://www.seakayak.ws/kayak/kayak.nsf/NavigationList/NT0000BE3E
Sea Recovery Marine desalinators for boats Crystal Sea 12v or 24v or 110v models P.O. Box 2560 Gardena, California 90247-0560 Tel: 1-310-637-3400 Website: www.searecovery.com .

SOLAR WATER HEATERS
King Solar Brands are excellent: www.kingsolar.com
Progressivtube: PO Box 3887, Sarasota, Fl 34230 Tel: (941) 953-2177
http://www.solardirect.com/swh/pt/pt1/why-progressivTube/why-progressivtube.htm or Abraham Solar Equipment.
Solahart USA Self contained storage tank, easy to install. Solahart 939 South, 48th Street #207, Tempe, AZ 85281 Tel: 602-967-6785, 800-233-7652. http://www.solahart.com/default.asp?V-DOC-ID=1
Solar Works, Inc. Roof mounted panel systems--large http://www.solar-works.com/ 64 Main Street, Montpelier, VT 05602 Tel: 802-223-7804 or 800-339-7804 (VT).

EVACUATED TUBE COLLECTORS (The best, and most high-tech)
Thermomax Evacuated Tube Collectors: 5560 Sterrett Place, Suite 115, Columbia, MD 21044 Tel: (410) 997-0778 URL: www.thermomax.com . This company has wide experience in joining a solar water heating system with a wood heating backup system into a hydronic floor-heated home.

SOLAR WATER PURIFIER
Sol*Saver Solar Water Pasteurizer Safe Water Systems 2800 Woodlawn Drive, Suite 131, Honolulu, Hawaii 96822 Tel: 808-539-3937 website: www.safewatersystems.com (they also have a wood burning water purifier).

SUN POWERED COOLING
Solar Powered Evaporative Coolers: "Solar Chill" by PB solar Solacool by Advantage Solar: http://www.advantagesolar.com/solacool.htm

SOLARIUM, ADD-ON GREENHOUSES
Durango Solariums, Durango Co, (970) 385-4561. There are similar custom solarium builders in every major city. http://durangosolariums.com/welcome.php

SOLAR GREENHOUSE VENT OPENERS
Thermofor, http://www.greenhouses-etc.net/equipment/solar-vents.htm
Bayless Mk-7 or XL from A Gardener's Resource, P. O. Box 85072, Tucson, Arizona 85754 Tel: (520) 792-8023 URL: www.greenhousesupplies.com .

SOLAR FANS, BLOWERS, COOLERS
The Sustainable Village: http://www.thesustainablevillage.com/products/display.do

SURVIVAL EQUIPMENT

HIGH SECURITY SHELTER

SEVERE COLD WEATHER CLOTHING
PALS SYSTEM --the very best in extreme cold weather clothing. Available in economical kits or ready-made suits (you add the outer shell by buying high quality Goretex outerwear. contact: PST (Preparedness and Survival Training Institute) in Utah at (801) 785-6027. Ask for the Inner Thermal Lining Kits. They also have a complete series of preparedness training videos on the clothing system and all other aspects of survival. Excellent. Jim Phillip's website is www.jimsway.com

TOOLS
Harbor Freight Tools: Deep discounted tools, quality is not the best, but improving every year--mostly Chinese or Taiwanese. Retail stores in all western States plus Lexington, Kentucky. Info: www.harborfreight.com . Call for printed catalog, 1-800- 423-2567.

TRANSPORTATION EQUIPMENT

ELECTRIC BICYCLES
Plans to Convert a Mountain Bike: $29 from Bill Gerosa, Convergence Tech., Inc., 12-6 Foxwood Drive, Pleasantville, NY 10570 Website: www.econvergence.net/emb.htm Tel: 914-773-6749
ZAP Power System: add-on package to motorize a mountain bike. Can still pedal with this system. ZAP SX Rear Range 15 miles with SX and 8 miles with DX. Has regenerative charging of battery while going downhill and pedaling. Can buy their "Electric Cruiser" bicycle ready and a ready made mountain bike. http://www.zapworld.com/ProductDetail.aspx?id=1500
Charger Bicycles: Electric bike designed from ground up with the latest innovative technology - multi option pedal assist system, dual chain, 20 mile range. http://www.electric-bikes.com/charger.htm
US Pro Drive (Currie Technology - used in Schwinn Bikes) Van Nuys, CA 91406 Tel: (818) 947-0366. Here's a direct-drive adaptive system with a variable speed controller. The direct drive system mounts on the rear hub of most 26" bicycles and weighs 6 lbs. The battery shell locks. Most people change out the awkward thumb throttle to a twist grip type http://etxcur.accpaconline.com/izipbikepage.html
EV Rider, Inc., 1060 Commerce Boulevard, North, Sarasota, Florida 34243 USA Toll-Free: 888-RIDEREV(743-3738) Fax: 941-351-2699, http://www.evrider.com . Mostly electric powered wheeled carts, but also have a folding electric bike: http://www.evrider.com/folding-bikw.htm
Electrobike, Inc. Ready to go bike with 20 mile range: http://www.electrobike.com/html/pro-jazz.html

ELECTRIC VEHICLE CONVERSIONS
This is the most economical way to get an electric vehicle. Convert a pickup or van to electric use with batteries and solar panels and have a short-range, reliable commute vehicle when gas becomes unavailable. Maximum range is typically 40 miles. The most experienced one stop shop for all necessary items is ELECTRO AUTOMOTIVE in California: www.electroauto.com or P.O. Box 1113, Felton Ca 95018-1113.

MILITEC-1 DRY LUBE FOR WEAPONS
http://www.militec1.com/

MILITEC-1 OIL ADDITIVE
I think this is the best oil additive for all types of engines/transmissions - proven to double the life of an engine: 16 Oz bottle (Half a bottle added to engine oil every 15,000 miles) http://www.militec1.com/

HIGH SECURITY SHELTER

REDLINE OIL PRODUCTS

REDLINE Simply the best racing oils available. Too expensive for me, since I use Militec-1 anyway, I don't feel I need the pricy oil. But I do use their transmission fluids. In a long term crisis, I want the longest life out of the transmission, and these special fluids have proven to be at least twice as good as normal hypoid oil. These are products primarily for manual transmission and differentials. I use 2 oz of Militec-1 in automatic transmission for protection. http://www.redlineoil.com/ Available online all over the www.

HIGH PERFORMANCE OIL FILTERS

AMSOIL http://www.amsoil.com/prod.html MSOIL INC. AMSOIL Building, Superior, Wisconsin 54880 Phone: (715) 392-7101. Amsoil makes a full range of very high performance synthetic oils and the best oil filter systems around.

WATER PURIFICATION/FILTERING EQUIPMENT

OXYGEN BASED WATER PURIFIERS

Aerobic K07 potassium based water purifier (about $20 each retail, local health food stores) Only buy the potassium based liquid with the "K" http://www.aerobiclife.com/

WATER FILTERS

Aquasana Uses high tech filters, low replacement price, lasts longest. Also, shower filters and multiple installation choices. best price: http://www.aquasana.com/catalog.cfm

Big Blue 20" is the best type of whole house filter. Has UV sterilization as well. Good prices at http://www.purewaterexpress.com/

WEAPONS

BOWIE KNIFE: Western Cutlery 9-1/2" blade Available at local knife shops that carry Western Cutlery products. Here's a pic: http://www.afterknife.com/western-cutlery-ww49-western-bowie-knife-95-in-p-454354050.html

MAG-NA-PORT ARMS - recoil reduction mod to weapons. 41302 Executive Dr., Mt. Clemens, MI 48045 Tel: 1-313-469-6727. http://www.magnaport.com/company.html

MAG-SAFE AMMO: Special penetrating shotgun type ammo for auto weapons. Awesome and deadly stuff. http://www.magsafeonline.com/

TRITICON glowing night sights: Armson, 1-313-553-4960. http://armson1.stores.yahoo.net/

DILLON Reloading Press: best of the progressive reloading presses. http://www.dillonprecision.com/ .

SILENT .22 AMMO: CCI brand .ww CB CAP cartridges - at most gun shops.

Williams Trigger Specialties - smooth trigger mods RR 1, Box 26-G, White Heath, Il 61884, Tel: 1-217-762-7377. http://www.soldierstuff.com/wts/

WATER POWER

LARGE HYDRO-ELECTRIC SYSTEMS

Hydro West Group, Inc. Manufacturer, service, large hydro-powered electric generators, complete system design (50 kW), microhydro electric generators, hydro energy components, hydro turbines. Address: 1422 130th Avenue N.E., Bellevue, WA 98166 Telephone: (425) 455-0234Web Site: http://hydrowest.com/ ,

HIGH SECURITY SHELTER

American Hydro Corporation For big projects. Custom design and manufactured upgrades for existing hydroturbines to boost output by 10 to 50%. Service : system design and installation. http://www.ahydro.com/

MEDIUM-SIZED HYDRO
Canyon Industries, Inc. Builds and engineers pelton and cross-flow turbines for medium head hydro conditions. Good hands-on experience. Call Dan New (360) 592-5552. P O Box 574 HP, Deming, WA 98244. URL: http://www.canyonhydro.com/

MICRO-HYDRO
Harris Pelton Turbines High head turbines (200-600 vertical feet of drop) 2, 3 or 4, nozzle designs. Abraham Solar Equipment.
Turgo Pelton Wheels - slightly better than Harris units: from Abraham Solar Equipment.

WIND POWER
WIND GENERATORS
Best of the Small Windchargers:

AIR 403- costs about $550 for the new 400 watt machine (installation is cheap and easy because this system is so small and portable). Abraham Solar 1-800-222-4727 or http://www.etaengineering.com/windpower/air-x-vs-403.shtml
Best of the Medium sized Windchargers:

WHISPER Corp. builds excellent units from 600 watts to 4500 watts - cost all below $2.00 a watt. Widely available online. Sample: http://www.advancepower.net/wind.htm

WINDMILLS FOR WATER WELLS
Dean Bennett Supply (many types) Toll Free: 800-621-4291. http://www.deanbennett.com/
Aeromotor: http://www.aermotorwindmill.com/Index.asp

APPENDIX B

EMERGENCY PREPAREDNESS RECOMMENDATIONS AND STOCKPILING LIST

The following preparedness list is intended to make sure that each family has a least the essentials to survive any general or local disaster that may close off or restrict food and water supplies for up to a year. Supplies are also included to help each family have on hand limited materials to make temporary repairs to their residence, and to be able to have emergency heating and cooking facilities without access to public power.

The following groups of recommendations are priority listed to help each person or family allocate limited funds first to the essentials of preparedness (level one first). This does not mean that the items in the later groups are less important. Some are more costly and should only be purchased after the essential items in earlier groups. Higher level categories also increase the amount of stored food products since the first two levels are for short term emergencies. This is only a general list for the average person. Feel free to improvise and adjust according to your own needs and circumstances and your own assessment of future threats.

LEVEL ONE: Short-term 72 hr. emergency where one is required to leave home with less than a few minutes notice, such as in a fire, storm, or area evacuation. Pack into travel bags and store in or near your vehicles, but out of high heat, if possible.

Travel bags: one small backpack, duffel bag or medium sports bag per person, plus one large duffel bag for family use.
Individual Equipment for each pack:

Clothing:
- 2 pair socks, warm, padded
- 1 pair old tennis shoes
- 1 pair pants, shirt, 1 change of underwear
- 1 old coat (light but with insulation)
- 1 stretch hat to cover ears
- 1 pair of insulating gloves

Equipment:
- 1 military style quilted lightweight blanket (poncho liner)
- 1 space blanket (Mylar-foil backed plastic sheet for heat retention)
- 1 6' x 6' sheet of plastic for a rain tarp
- 1 ½ litre Mylar plastic water bottle
- 2 ziplock type bags for food
- 1 small candle, 2 packs of matches in ziplock bag
- 1 small camp knife
- 1 small tube of sun screen
- 1 small first aid kit with cloth athletic tape, band aids and antiseptic
- 1 small insect repellent
- 1 small whistle with a neck cord
- 1 pack facial tissues
- 1 cyalume light stick, 3 chemical hand warmer packages
- 2 spoons, one metal large, one plastic
- 1 hand towel, small motel size soap, an old toothbrush
- 1 small bottle Aerobic K07 oxygenated water purifier

Food:
- 7 MRE food packs
- 1 small bottle vitamins: mix in some 500 mg natural Vitamin C tablets with a multivitamin
- 7individually packages granola bars, a few strips of beef jerky in a sealed bag
- 1 small pack of dried fruit

DOCUMENT PACK: We recommend that you keep important documents in a small, fire resistant portable safe (Sentry brand etc.). Keep it in a hidden location but where you can grab it and run.

HIGH SECURITY SHELTER

FAMILY PACK: These are group use items that you don't want to pack for each individual. There is some duplication here with individual packs, for safety reasons.

Water: One gallon water in sealed Mylar Pack (Emergency Essentials has them)
1 plastic collapsible container for refilling with water
3 cone type coffee filters for filtering water
1 bottle K07 Oxygen water purifier

Food: 2 packages "cup of soup" per person
2 ziplock bags full of ground wheat type cereal.
1 large bag of mixed dehydrated fruit
1 large package Beef jerky
1 Granola bar per person per day
1 freezer bag instant powdered milk
1 MRE pack per person per day

Equipment:
2 "canned heat" solid fuel with mini grill to support pot over heat
2 camp cook pots, nested inside each other, stainless steel (not aluminum)
1 Sharp Kitchen knife, 5-7 inches
1 package paper towels
1 package plastic bowls, plates and cups
1 package assorted plastic utensils
1 small bottle of detergent and a small Scotch brand scrub pad
2 hand towels and assorted rags
1 bath towel
2 sleeping bags capable of being zipped together
1 signal mirror and one mini pack of signal flares (boating store)
50 feet of mountaineer rope with a couple of caribiners and a pulley
1 large rain tarp with grommet holes
100 feet of parachute type cord
1 hatchet, small packet assorted nails
1 folding camp saw
3 chemical light sticks
1 water resistant LED flashlight
1 12 volt portable light with cig lighter plug and long cord for working on car
1 bottle insect repellant
1 family sized first aid kit
1 portable SW/AM/FM radio with batteries
1 set of waterproof matches, candle
1 roll toilet paper
1 large spray can pepper spray for security

LEVEL TWO: Storage for one month emergency supplies, at home, in addition to Level One supplies

Water: Store 1 quart of water per person per day (treat static water storage with K07 oxygenated purifier—not chlorine, and store water in a dark cool space.

Food: 25 lbs/person wheat (sealed in plastic buckets or double poly bags)
4 lbs/person powdered milk (non instant, so you will need a blender)
10-20 lbs rice per person
1 large container of sea salt
1 reg. size container Baking Powder
1- 5 lb can of honey (preferably raw, unfiltered)
1 gallon can of vegetable cooking oil
1 large can of dehydrated powdered butter
1 month supply of normal canned goods, condiments, and foods you normally eat
Fresh garlic bulbs (or gel caps for long-term storage)
Vitamins: Vit. C (natural, 500mg size) Multiple, Kelp tablets, Mag/Calcium, B-complex, E.
Yeast for Baking bread---keep cool.

Supplies:
2 extra packs of light bulbs each in wattages of 40, 60, 75, 100
1 case of toilet paper, paper towels
1 package of garbage bags
1 package aluminum foil, plastic wrap
1 package of medium and large freezer bags
1 large bottle of detergent, and of household cleaner, and one of disinfectant
1 large container of liquid laundry detergent
5 bars of hand soap
4 rolls of duct tape, 2 rolls of strapping tape
Glue: white glue, epoxy, super glue, contact cement, vinyl shoe goo
1 roll of cord or twine
Needles, thread, including some heavy-duty curved needles
Large pack of alkaline batteries in AAA, AA, C, D.
Extra flashlight bulbs for every type you own
2 5 gallon plastic fuel containers, filled with fuel plus stabilizer
1 large family first aid kit with a good manual, scissors, tapes, splints, tweezers, thermometer, etc

Equipment:
1 mountain bicycle per person who can ride, plus repair kits
2 oil lamps with extra fuel
2 5-gallon propane cylinders w/propane camp stove and lantern
2 LED flashlights or lanterns
1 adjustable wrench, large, for turning off gas valve in an earthquake
Wheat grinder, electric for flour and manual for cracked wheat cereal
Electric blender
1 package of coffee filters for filtering water

HIGH SECURITY SHELTER

Repair Tools and Supplies:

1 shovel and pick
1 long pry bar, 1 hydraulic jack
1 hammer and 10 lbs of nails, 16d and 8d
2 lbs of "grabber" screws (3/4" 1", 1-1/2", 2-1/2")
1 wood cutting bow saw
Sheets of ½" plywood for boarding up windows
1 large roll of 6ml white plastic for covering broken windows or fixing roof
4 lbs plastic top roofing nails for plastic
Tool box with assorted pliers, screwdrivers, wrenches etc for fixing things
Plumbing repair fittings to seal or splice broken plumbing, depending on type

LEVEL THREE: For long-term disaster of up to a year or two in duration. The following should be stored in addition to levels one and two. It takes considerable time to collect and store this kind of materials and equipment. Do not wait till disaster is imminent and people are rushing to buy.

Water: 1 extra water tank inside the house, plumbed in-line with your existing water heater---thus it always stays fresh. Remember to turn off the inlet valve after an earthquake to prevent contaminated dirty water from entering your storage and hot water tanks.

Food: 300 lbs of wheat per person, sealed in plastic buckets or double poly bags
20 lbs per person of non-instant powdered milk
100 lbs per person dried beans
100 lbs per person milled rice (brown rice is healthier but must be keep refrigerated)
3 lbs per person sea salt or unrefined mineral salt
2 lbs yeast and 1 lb baking powder
10 lbs per person honey
1 gal per person vegetable oil (do not use hydrogenated oils)
Assorted bulk containers of spices
50 lbs per person of potato flakes, or real potatoes if you have a cellar
2 gallons dried onions
2 gallons mayonnaise. Can substitute salted oil if necessary for butter.
Heritage seeds for planting a garden

Equipment: these are somewhat minimal, but essential to start with.
Food canner, with bottles, rings and lids (several hundred)
Generator (5000 watt recommended with 55 gallon drum of fuel w/ barrel pump)
2 extra car batteries with solar panel for charging
Portable 1000 watt inverter for converting battery voltage to 110 volts
1 wood burning stove if you live in a cold climate, with a winter's supply of wood
Manual clothes wringer (auto parts store: buy a Chamois wringer)
Full array of garden tools

Supplies: Increase all in the Level Two list to a two year's supply

Spare Parts: Stock up on things that you cannot easily home manufacture or repair: fan belts, fuses, vacuum cleaner bags, anti-freeze, oil, oil filters, brake fluid, brake pads, lights, bulbs, bicycle tubes, paper pens, and critical supplies necessary for your business.

Money: Keep 3 months cash on hand outside of banks, safely hidden. Gold and Silver coins too.

APPENDIX C

SUGGESTED BARTER ITEMS

BARTER CRITERIA:
1. Highly desirable and needed by a large segment of the population
2. Durable: must maintain its value in storage and in handling
3. Divisible: allows one to barter in small or large increments
4. Recognizable and easily verifiable without expert opinion.
5. Portable: good barter items can be carried away, stored or hidden with ease
6. Scarce: things that are plentiful now often become scarce in a crisis
7. Can't be easily home manufactured—lending to scarcity when production fails

As you will see, most of these items are things you would want to store anyway (except the addictive items), so storing for barter assures you won't run out. Don't forget to store items for you business or to barter with other business.

CLEANSERS, SOAPS (liq detergents, laundry soap, bleach, disinfectants, hand cleaner, alcohol)
MEDICINES (pain killers, anti-fungals, antibiotics,)
VITAMINS AND MINERALS (Buy only natural ones—not synthetic from the pharmaceuticals)
ESSENTIAL FLUIDS (gasoline, diesel, alcohol, anti-freeze, paint thinner, acetone, brake fluid)
CLOTHING ITEMS (Nylon stockings, socks, underwear, boots and shoes)
WEAPONS, AMMUNITION (all common calibers, esp .22 which cannot be reloaded)
RELOADING SUPPLIES (powder, primer, cases, bullets)
PAPER (copy paper, envelopes)
WRITING INSTRUMENTS (pens, pencils, felt tip pens, markers)
CAR PARTS (fan belts, spark plugs, oil filters, tires, batteries)
BICYCLE PARTS (repair kits, inner tubes, and tires)
LEGAL ADDICTIVE SUBSTANCES (cigarettes, coffee, liquor)
REPAIR ITEMS (glue, screws, nails, bolts, nuts, tape)
ELECTRICAL (batteries, bulbs, small testers, wire, wire nuts)
ESSENTIAL HOUSEHOLD ITEMS (light bulbs, canning lids, jars, needles, thread, zippers, buttons)
STRING, CORD, ROPE
GARDEN SEEDS AND FERTILIZER
KNIVES, RAZOR BLADES, DISPOSABLE SHAVERS
SANDPAPER, FILES, GRINDING WHEELS
MONEY: (Silver dollars, junk silver coins---dimes, quarters)
MATCHES, BOTTLED PROPANE, KEROSENE, WOOD PELLETS
CHEMICALS (Insect repellant, weed control, insect killer---esp. during an infestation)

APPENDIX D

WATER STORAGE AND PURIFICATION

Your most critical storage need is water. Water cannot be rationed very effectively when you run short. Even slow dehydration causes many adverse health effects. If the amount you store does not last, you will have to obtain water from whatever source available, filter it, and purify it to be suitable for drinking.

STORAGE AMOUNTS:

Because water is needed in fairly large quantities, it is not easy to store all you need, indefinitely, at least within the confines of a shelter. Critical supplies of drinking water should be stored in the shelter and additional supplies should be available from other tanks or cisterns outside the shelter. The following amounts are recommended:

Body maintenance and cooking water: 1 pint/day/person (cool weather)
1 quart/day/person (hot weather)
1 gallon/day/person (hot weather, heavy labor)
To maintain comfort, one must double these amounts.

Wash Water: 1 quart/day/person (washing with a wet cloth only)
1 quart/day/person (dishes and hand washing clothes)

Shower/bathing: showering into a tub uses the least water, and the residue can be recycled for toilet flushing. A water saver shower head uses 1-2 gallons per minute under pressure. Run water only while wetting down and rinsing off.

STORAGE SOURCES:

1. Hot water tank: open a faucet at some higher level in the house and then the drain valve (usually a hose bib) at the bottom of the tank. These are low to the ground, so supply a short garden hose to ease filling higher containers.

2. Cold water lines: You can also get a gallon or more of water out of the residue left in house lines. Drain from the lowest cold water outlet after opening faucets and bath fixtures up high.

3. Toilet Tank: The water in the toilet tank above the toilet (not the bowl water) is OK to use (unless someone places odor reducing chemicals inside).

4. Rain water from roof: Collect in barrels at each downspout. Filter out any leaves or dust from the roof. A permanent rain water collection system can be established if one has an underground cistern to channel the water to and a sand filled barrel to act as a filter.

5. Other free running water outside: streams, puddles, rivers. Be prepared to use them all. Remember that bad odors are a sign of bacteria. Filter with a coffee filter and then boil for at least 20 minutes.

HIGH SECURITY SHELTER

ADDITIONAL STORAGE: (prepared in advance)
1. Glass bottles. Use empty canning jars to store water. The disadvantage with this method is that glass can break in an earthquake. Store on shelves with bungee cord restraints to keep jars on the shelves. It is also a good practice to place strips of cardboard between rows of bottles. Bottles should be sterilized before storing water in them, and should have 3 drops of oxygen purifier put in them if not hot packed.

2. Plastic Bottles. Do not use empty milk jugs. This low grade plastic absorbs odors and breaks down in light. Use Mylar bottles instead---like two-litre pop or water bottles. They are nearly unbreakable and do not degrade over time. PVC plastics should be avoided as they leach some chemical odors.

3. Heavy duty storage barrels: Use only the types made for potable water (usually blue in color). Use K07 drops in water so that you don't have to rotate your stock. Remember that water weights 8.4 lbs per gallon. Watch where you put this kind of weight. Once filled, a 55 gallon drum is pretty hard to move.

GENERAL PRECAUTIONS ON WATER NEEDS IN A CRISIS
1. Beware of high levels of Chlorine, which leave TMH toxic residues. Do not drink swimming pool water without a KDF filter and boiling to remove chorine residue.
2. Do not drink salt water under any conditions
3. If you are severely dehydrated do not eat food unless it is succulent. Most food takes more water from your body for digestion than it provides.
5. If rationing water, drink enough to restore strength so you can keep moving. Drinking too little at a time will not allow you to keep moving in order to find more water, or to avoid dehydration.
6. If surviving in hot areas, travel when cool or at night. Lay down in the shade during the day. Sitting in the hot sun will not preserve life---better to keep moving slowly. Use sweat effectively by keeping lightweight shirts on your body to both shield from the sun and prolong the effectiveness of sweating.

WATER FILTRATION AND PURIFICATION

SETTLING: This is the preferable way to remove gross sediment without clogging filters. Allow 12 to 24 hours and then pour off or siphon off clear liquid without disturbing sediment.

FILTERING: moderately effective:

Coffee filters: Use one or more filters over the rim of a large-mouth jar (gallon jar is best) and screw on lid with center portion cut out. Replace top layer when clogged or too slow.

Sand filters: Use two 5 gallon plastic pails. Punch holes in one, put in a 1" layer of gravel, then a cloth, then 6" of fine sand. You can also use diatomaceous earth, aquarium media, or charcoal. Finally place another cloth over the sand as a cleanable filter of gross material. Place this filter bucket inside the other clean bucket. Pour in dirty water and it will come out fairly clean. Boil the resultant liquid. No filter is fine enough for virus.

PURIFICATION, STERILIZATION
BOILING: Boiling vigorously for 20 minutes as a minimum. Add 1 minute per thousand feet of altitude. Pressure cooking at 15 lbs pressure is even more effective at reaching a higher temperature faster.
Boiling is more effective with water that has cloudy particles in it because it can kill bacteria embedded in particles that may escape chemical action. When cooled, aerate water by pouring it back and forth in two containers vigorously.

OXYGEN: Non-toxic sodium or potassium based liquids with high doses of electrically bonded oxygen are the most promising water purifiers because they only kill bad bacteria and are harmless to humans in the proper dosage. The most popular stabilized oxygen product is K07 from Aerobic Life Industries in Phoenix, AZ. The dosage of drops per gallon must be increased from the basic 10 drops/gallon depending on how bacteria is present. 32 drops per gallon will handle most cases. Add oxygen drops and shake, then let sit for 20 minutes. K07 is also drinkable in diluted form of 10 drops per glass of water and will attack bad bacteria in the stomach and intestine---great for a case of diarrhea.

CHEMICAL PURIFIERS:
IODINE CRYSTALS: Iodine in crystalline form is the only fully effective non-oxygen based chemical treatment that you can rely on. It kills everything in water. It has an indefinite shelf life, but it is highly toxic if you ingest the crystals. Thus, it is not marketed commercially. Ask for USP resublimated iodine crystals at any chemical supply house. Do not touch or handle the crystals with your bare hands, or burns can result. Place 1 or 2 grams of the crystals in a 1 oz bottle, add water, and shake for a minute or two. Add one tablespoon of this liquid (not the crystals from the bottom) per gallon. Shake and let stand for 15 or 20 minutes. It's not hard to do.

IODINE TABLETS: Tetraglycine Hyperiodide is very effective against bacteria but only partially against Giardia. Additionally, it has a fairly short shelf life, especially in the sun or heat. The tablets are gray in color when new, and turn yellowish as they get old. It takes one or two tablets per quart depending on the condition of the water. There is an aftertaste.

LIQUID IODINE: Tincture of iodine is not very effective but 30 drops per gallon will kill most bacteria as well as add a very bad taste to the water. It is not very effective in drinkable doses against Giardia.

LIQUID BLEACH (Hypochlorite): Use only if the bleach is hypochlorite. Other types are toxic, especially the granular forms of Chlorine. Hypochlorite isn't healthy either, and neither is it very effective against the worst bacteria. But it is better than nothing if that is all you have. I still cringe at how often bleach is touted as the primary purifier recommended by government and amateur camping experts. Add 8 drops per gallon and shake well and let stand for 30 minutes. Aerate and let stand in an open bowl in the sun, or boil to get rid of the Chlorine. All Chlorines leave Trimethylhaline (TMH) toxins as they react with contaminants, just like public water supplies.

APPENDIX E

INSTALLATION OF RESERVE WATER TANK

Whether you have a gas or electric water heater, you can add another water heater next to it, room permitting. If you have gas, install an electric water heater beside it to have a backup with a different fuel type, and vice versa---although you may have to install a propane heater if gas isn't available. Under normal conditions, the new water heater has the power or fuel turned off so that it merely acts as a pre-heater (to room temperature) and a reserve water supply. Pre-heating takes place slowly as the incoming cold water first goes through the auxiliary tank and then into the active water heater, where it slowly warms up to room temperature, saving energy in the total water heating process. The multiple valve and pipe connections in the accompanying illustration are intended to allow the owner to use one or both tanks separately or together.

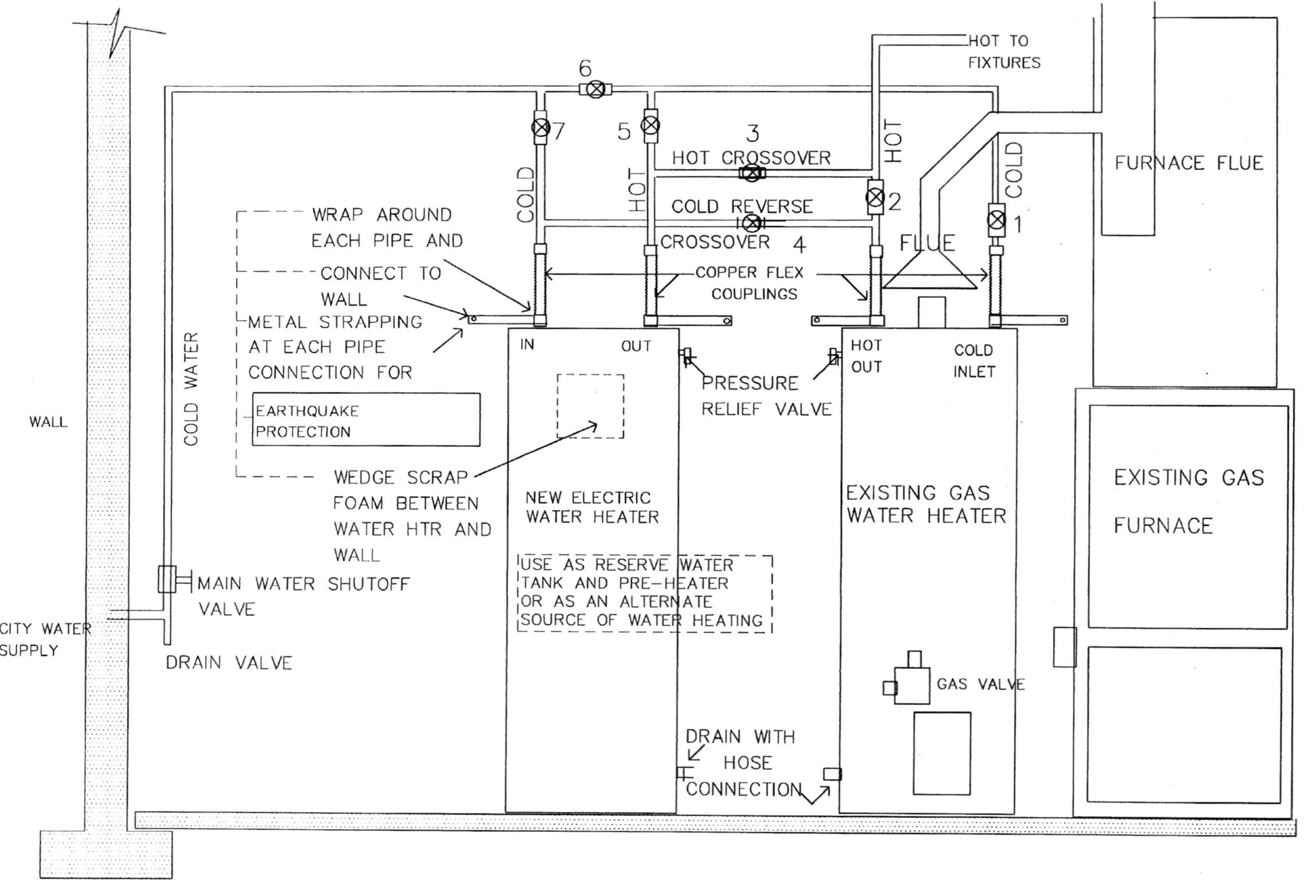
HOT TO FIXTURES
FURNACE FLUE
6
7
5
3
HOT CROSSOVER
HOT
COLD
HOT
COLD REVERSE
CROSSOVER 4
2
COLD
1
FLUE
COPPER FLEX COUPLINGS
WRAP AROUND EACH PIPE AND
CONNECT TO WALL
METAL STRAPPING AT EACH PIPE CONNECTION FOR
EARTHQUAKE PROTECTION
WEDGE SCRAP FOAM BETWEEN WATER HTR AND WALL
IN
OUT
HOT OUT
COLD INLET
PRESSURE RELIEF VALVE
NEW ELECTRIC WATER HEATER
EXISTING GAS WATER HEATER
EXISTING GAS FURNACE
USE AS RESERVE WATER TANK AND PRE-HEATER OR AS AN ALTERNATE SOURCE OF WATER HEATING
GAS VALVE
DRAIN WITH HOSE CONNECTION
COLD WATER
WALL
MAIN WATER SHUTOFF VALVE
CITY WATER SUPPLY
DRAIN VALVE
ADDING A RESERVE WATER SUPPLY

APPENDIX F

BUILDING A CISTERN

Building a rain water collection system and storing it in a below ground cistern is a very cost effective way to get one to two thousand gallons of storage that will stay fresh for years at a time. The accompanying drawing showing the construction and installation of the cistern should be self-explanatory. The rain water collection barrels, which act as filters, should be at least half way out of the ground and surrounded by some type of shrubbery or decorative planter box to inhibit freezing. The height out of the ground is to allow for gravity flow to the cistern without having to bury the cistern too deeply (the top of the cistern must be below the bottom of the filter barrel). If you have a basement, the bottom of the cistern must be a couple of feet above the basement floor to allow for sufficient gravity flow to a basement outlet valve.

You may wish to join the outflow of two or more downspouts to maximize the collection of water if you live in a dry climate, or anticipate drought conditions. You should provide a manhole for the top of the cistern for checking on the condition of the water, or to clean out the cistern if necessary. You should also provide a 4" overflow pipe exiting near the top and leading to daylight with a screen on the end to keep insects or vermin from crawling up into the cistern. A drowned mouse is not good for water purity.

The outlet pipe from the bottom of the cistern, connecting to the house should be drilled a couple of inches from the bottom and sealed with silicone. PVC pipe is adequate. Make sure that any separating walls in the cistern are drilled through at the bottom so that water will completely drain out.

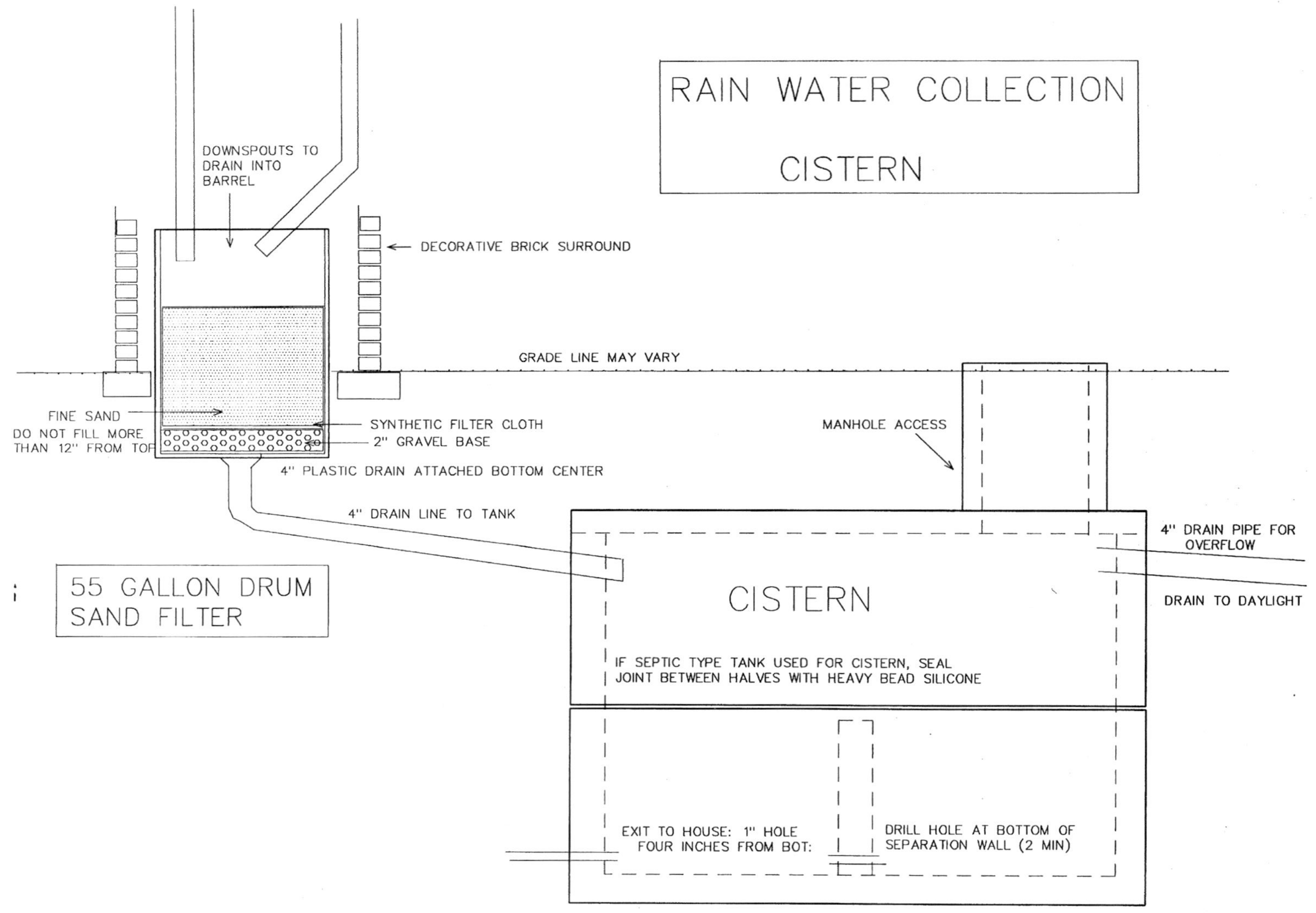
RAIN WATER COLLECTION
CISTERN
DOWNSPOUTS TO DRAIN INTO BARREL
DECORATIVE BRICK SURROUND
GRADE LINE MAY VARY
FINE SAND
DO NOT FILL MORE THAN 12" FROM TOP
SYNTHETIC FILTER CLOTH
2" GRAVEL BASE
4" PLASTIC DRAIN ATTACHED BOTTOM CENTER
MANHOLE ACCESS
4" DRAIN LINE TO TANK
4" DRAIN PIPE FOR OVERFLOW
55 GALLON DRUM SAND FILTER
CISTERN
DRAIN TO DAYLIGHT
IF SEPTIC TYPE TANK USED FOR CISTERN, SEAL JOINT BETWEEN HALVES WITH HEAVY BEAD SILICONE
EXIT TO HOUSE: 1" HOLE FOUR INCHES FROM BOT:
DRILL HOLE AT BOTTOM OF SEPARATION WALL (2 MIN)

APPENDIX G

Nuclear Radiation Protection Procedures

Contrary to popular media misrepresentations, the chances of surviving a nuclear explosion are very good if you are not within the actual blast zone. Your greater threat after surviving the fallout will actually come from the accompanying social unrest and the tyranny Federal Emergency Management Agency (FEMA) personnel who will attempt to force rural residents to provide shelter for city evacuees as a last ditch "civil defense" maneuver. Supposing that you have prepared yourself for fallout protection with a suitable security shelter, there are certain basic training procedures that you should implement in order to ensure that the family will be able to use that shelter and its equipment when needed.

1. Develop a plan for getting the family back together if separated when the blast occurs. This should involve designating alternative locations for shelter in every part of the normal vicinity of their everyday activities. This may include other homes (with basements) of friends and acquaintances, and even businesses that may have basement space for temporary shelter. Whatever places or persons you select for them to meet for safety, make sure your children always have a package **post-it notes** with them and a pencil. Train them that whenever they leave their last known position (school or a friends house) they should write on the post-it note where they are going, what time, and with whom. Have them write on the side of the note with the sticky edge so they can stick the note to a window in the front of the building or house near the main door, so it will be visible to you or the authorities and won't be blown away as it would be if on the outside. This tactic is essential in helping you track your missing children. Don't depend on cell phones to get through in a crisis when everyone is trying to use the phone. Better to text a message than call. If you live in a high risk military target area, additional warning and communications equipment should include a home pager system for each member of the family. These are very inexpensive.

2. Some basic training should be given in the short term use of expedient shelters. These are very difficult for anyone to accomplish who is not an adult or who does not have tools for digging, but the knowledge of their construction and use may buy a little time until a child can be picked up and brought to a better shelter.

3. First aid and fallout decontamination procedures should be part of every family member's training.

4. Training should encompass operating and living in your security shelter. This should include operation of ventilation, lighting and generating systems, security and communications equipment, food preparation, sanitation, and monitoring of fallout levels with the radiation meters

5. Teach family members about certain warning signals which may allow them to prepare in advance of a nuclear threat – such as indications the nation has received an EMP strike. All electricity goes down and there are no TV or radio stations on the air. Visible signs are a fireball in the distance, giving advance warning of approaching radiation fallout.

6. Prepare a multiple contingency evacuation plan from your city if it is a primary target area (for use when you have advance warning). You should have as many alternatives as possible which allow you to go around or over the massive traffic jams that may result. Only off-road vehicles, bicycles, and motorcycles will get through on the ground, as long as no fallout is in the air. Those who are pilots may even wish to provide an contingency airlift out of the area. Nothing beats having your own

private airstrip on your property. Others may have access to some resort communities that have their own airstrips. Whatever you do, don't keep your plane at a highly regulated major airport with a control tower– they may well prohibit you from taking off or from even getting to your plane.

General Precautions If You are Near a Blast Area

Never look out a window at an explosion; the oncoming shock wave will burst the window into your face. Never look at the light of a blast as it is full of instantaneous radiation energy. Move quickly into a hall of room without windows. Wait two minutes for a blast wave to arrive before trying to go outdoors to enter an exterior shelter. The initial blast wave travels about one mile in the first five seconds before it begins slowing down. If no blast wave reaches you within two minutes, the blast is over 25 miles away and you will not be hurt by direct blast effects. Persons 100 miles away may have to wait as long as 7-10 minutes before hearing the blast.

Children who are away from home when a blast occurs must try to get home if at all possible before the fallout comes raining down – especially if they have no place to find expedient shelter (heavily reinforced concrete buildings, especially those with basements). Teach them that it makes no difference if they have to stay in a place without food and water, it is suicide to go outside and be exposed to fallout. You must be very strict about these instructions, for children don't usually do well when everyone around them is panicking. They must be especially warned about blindly following the instructions of teachers or other leaders who have no idea what to do in a nuclear situation. Teach them to sense which way and how strong the wind is blowing. This is their main way of telling how long they have till fallout reaches them.

If you are driving in a car when you see the flash of a nuclear weapon, you must stop immediately and get out of the direct view of the blast. The direct radiation from the blast is very strong and can put you over the limit of radiation exposure in a very few seconds. Even stopping and ducking down under the dash board is helpful. When you try to make it home, train yourself to avoid getting stuck in the massive traffic jams that surely will happen. Stick to the side streets and residential streets rather than the major thoroughfares. If you see a jam up ahead, turn off onto another street before you get trapped in the jam. If you have to stop, leave more space than usual to your front so you can turn your car around if necessary.

Above, all teach your children self-control and toughness. No amount of intellectual training will compensate for lack of self-control or toughness in a crisis---the time when each person has to make themselves do whatever necessary to get to safety and survive. You don't teach toughness without pressure---both mental and physical. That is why being permissive and soft spoken in your discipline as a parent is not always the best policy. When serious disciplinary problems arise, raise your voice and let them experience the confrontation and demands of immediate compliance. Don't be afraid to use some physical discipline when tantrums or outright rebellion arise.

Requiring them to control themselves, even when having fun, is part of good mental and spiritual training. Above all teach them to listen to conscience---especially those nervous feelings warning them that something is wrong, and those pushing feelings trying to get them to do something right, even when they don't feel like it. Discipline according to violations of conscience, not just rules, and the chances are they will get very good at listening to those divine promptings. Physical training that requires endurance is also a great way to develop toughness.

APPENDIX H

DESIGN AND CONSULTATION

TO ORDER Mr. Skousen's other books:

THE SECURE HOME (700 pages, $45) http://www.joelskousen.com/Secure/secure.html

STRATEGIC RELOCATION—North American Guide to Safe Places ($35) http://www.joelskousen.com/Strategic/strategic.html

Mr. Skousen also puts out a weekly analysis of world affairs called the **WORLD AFFAIRS BRIEF: Go to www.worldaffairsbrief.com or email him at editor@worldaffairsbrief.com for a sample copy.**

MR. SKOUSEN'S CONSULTATION AND CUSTOM DESIGN SERVICES

Mr. Skousen specializes in consulting on self-sufficient, secure, personal residences and retreats, including: site selection, contingency planning, self-sufficient living, and overall planning of the project. His son Andrew is a licensed structural engineer and takes care of the production of plans, or you can select your own local designer to work with Mr. Skousen's overall plan Almost any standard stock plan with a basement can be made secure and energy efficient. Mr. Skousen will, of course, advise you if he feels something you are planning to implement has serious drawbacks. That's what you pay him for. In general, self-sufficiency and security can be designed into a full range of styles, from classical to modern. He emphasizes the need to keep a low profile, and generally recommends that the finished product not draw undue attention to itself. In all of these areas, Mr. Skousen designs with the goal of complete integration of the applicable technical equipment you need to become more secure and self-sufficient.

HOW TO PROCEED **CONTACT MR. SKOUSEN BY EMAIL AT JOELS@JOELSKOUSEN.COM OR CALL HIM AT 801-224-4746 AND DESCRIBE YOUR SITUATION AND NEEDS. HIS FEES ARE STILL ONLY $60/HR, PRORATED BY THE MINUTE. SO, IF YOU TALK 20 MINUTES, IT'S ONLY $20.**

FEE SCHEDULE: TRAVEL AND ON-SITE CONSULTATION: **$500 PER DAY PLUS TRAVEL EXPENSES.**